Political Terror

Cold Warfare II

Dr. Patrick J. Pacalo,
Capt., Ph.D.

This book is dedicated to
the Victims of terror and
terrorism down through the
ages.

Table of Contents

Selected Quotes on

Cold War Era Terrorism

With the exception of Woodrow Wilson' s mention of terrorism in the Soviet Union in 1918, there are few remarks made before the Administration of Richard Nixon on the subject of terrorism. Global terrorism reared its head in the late 1960s; before that America and the rest of the world lived a charmed life in that respect. It is perhaps no coincidence that when advances in the televised media, and modern transportation coming of age occurred, that the phenomenon of global terrorism with its technology and complexity matured, and terrorist groups proliferated. Before the 1960s, terrorism was more brutal and widespread, as in the communist purges. Later it became more precise with more precise targets and methods, as in various PLO attacks.

"There are those who protest that if the verdict of democracy goes against them, democracy itself is at fault—who say that if they do not get their own way the answer is to burn a bus or bomb a building." Richard Nixon, September 16, 1970, Address at Kansas State University.

"International terrorism is not exclusively and Arab-Israeli problem; it is an international problem, which the United States has made a major international effort to combat. But a generation of frustration among displaced Palestinians has made the Middle East a particular focal point for such violence.... The recent murders of one Belgian and two American diplomats in Khartoum underscore the global dimension of the terrorist problem." Richard Nixon, May 3, 1973, From the Forth Annual Report to the Congress on US Foreign Policy.

"I call upon all nations to join in this vital endeavor. I particularly urge those countries which have not become parties to these conventions to do so.
"I hope that a new initiative against terrorism, as it affects innocent persons and disrupts the fabric of society, will be addressed at the current session of the United Nations General Assembly. The full force of world opinion and diplomatic action must be brought to bear on this threat to world peace and order."
Gerald R. Ford, October 10, 1976,
Statement on Signing the International Terrorism Prevention Bill.

"The murder of ABC correspondent Bill Stewart in Nicaragua is a tragedy for his family, his friends, and for freedom loving people everywhere.
"Bill Stewart was a dedicated and courageous journalist. At the time of his death, he was attempting to perform the highest duty of the American press: to inform the public on important issues of the day."
Jimmy Carter, June 28,1979, Telegram to ABC.

"There are skilled and professional terrorists out there right now, examining our vulnerabilities and building devices designed to kill Americans—lots of Americans. No matter what we do, we are going to be vulnerable." General P.X. Kelly, USMC Statement to the US Congress in 1983.

"There are no specific or definite threats that any of us know of here. We only know that worldwide there has been a call in a number of these terrorist groups for stepped-up violence. The term 'United States has been used as a potential target." Ronald Reagan, December 20, 1983, News Conference.

"The Legislation I am sending to the Congress is an important step in our war against terrorism. It will send a strong and vigorous message to friend and foe alike that the United States will not tolerate terrorist activity against its citizens or within its borders." Ronald Reagan, April 26, 1984
Message to the Congress Transmitting Proposed Legislation to Combat International Terrorism.

"We have been through a period in our history where we had what I would call terrorism, and it is probably before you were born, or maybe about that time. You remember the hijackings or airplanes in this country to go to Cuba? We forget that, we forget that we went through a rash of those hijackings…To hijack an airplane at gun point and instruct the pilot to go elsewhere, fly to Cuba, that's international terror. So we have been through that."
George H. W. Bush, May 28, 1989,
Q and A with Students: James Madison High School, Vienna, Virginia.

"…all of us policymakers from top to bottom underestimated the degree of terrorist threat which could be presented to our men and women in uniform, and they don't deserve that. They deserve the best possible decision making by us."
William Clinton, December 13, 1996,
At a News Conference Talking About the Bombing of the US Khobar Towers Building in Saudi Arabia.

"I can hear you. I can hear you. The rest of the world hears you. And the people who knocked these buildings down will hear all of us soon."
George W. Bush, September 14, 2001,
Impromptu Remarks at the World Trade Center Site in New York City.

Foreword and Acknowledgments

This book is a follow on to *Cold Warfare: A Compact History* which was published by the good people of Publish America in 2004. This book can be read after the more general Cold War history or it can be read alone. A series of books is planned on the subject of the Cold War. In the *Compact History* volume this author strove to get at the causes of the Cold War, and its often covert means. Additionally, that volume strove to point out that covert action was not new to the Cold War and that the roots of the Cold War were probably best described as being in the end of World War 1(1917-1918) rather than in the post-World War II period. There are a few historians out there who acknowledge the contribution to the ideology of 1918 and prior, but I think none as strong as in *Cold Warfare: A Compact History*. The essence of "cold warfare" is the covert, low-intensity and/or ideological nature of the fight.

1 would like to take a moment of the reader' s time here to explain why anyone would write books in this information technology age of computers, other devices, and the World Wide Web. In some ways this book is intended to show what can be done by using a blend of sources, primarily from a conventional library. Sometimes it seems that the book and all books are obsolete. This is so in many places today, including the legal profession as a prime example. Of course, the book has its advantages. Paper does not "crash." It is also easier on the eyes, more portable than most devices, and requires no batteries or WiFi technology to function properly. Finally, I believe that one can only gain so much depth from articles downloaded from a library's subscription of databases.

As for the issue of what this book is all about, *Cold Warfare II: Political Terrorism* seeks to look at that one aspect of the Cold War which brought the conflict home to so many around the world. Hostage-taking, aircraft and ship hijacking, abductions and murders, bombings, and events such as the machine-gunning of airports, are the types of events this volume examines. Like its predecessor it looks at the causes and contributing factors. Also like its predecessor, Volume II sees ideology as a primary motivator for the terrorist leadership. Poverty, abuse of rights, and land disputes often provided the recruits the terrorist groups and their supporters needed to exist. In some respects, the only purpose of this second book is to recount and make available, in one place, some of the facts of terrorism during the Cold War.

The examination gets somewhat more difficult when we try to fix responsibility for the terrorist acts that took place. Generally, the Soviets supported countries like those in the East Bloc, and Libya and Syria. Those countries in turn supported the terrorists with arms, money, and training. There are some notable cases, though, where it appears the Soviets became directly involved in the murderous business of terrorism. Terrorism in the Soviet system was not an exception, it was the rule. One only has to look at modern China to see that Marxism almost universally leads to the use of terrorism.

In this book there are two types of terrorism examined. First, the terrorism practiced by a government on its own people. Second, there is terrorism practiced by groups of individuals, as opposed to nations, towards some possible or nearly imaginary goal.

One could argue over whether the fight on America's part was just or not. The decades-long war on terrorism definitely soiled the USA's hands when it and its allies became involved in trying to defeat the terrorists. Here we see the Cold War era war on terrorism in the past tense. The post-9/11 war on terror continues to date and likely will for some time. Was the Cold War conflict worth the fight? Was the fight necessary? Fighting this aspect of the Cold War caused the denial of resources to other problems on a global basis. It is up to the reader to decide if it was right to fight rather than negotiate; sometimes both avenues were pursued at once. Clearly America had the right to fight back when its people and territory were attacked.

After the Cold War, with all its terrorist activities, America should have been ready for a 9/11/01 *during and after* the Cold War. Of course, many predicted, or better said, expected that America would suffer grievous harm to terrorism, possibly nuclear, biological, or chemical. Few would have predicted the craftiness and guile of 9/11/01. There were Cold War ties to 9/11, but to be clear, this is not a book about 9/11, or even its causes or precursors. In some unavoidable respects it is a book about terrorism *before* 9/11.

The Soviets duped many with their ideology. Many of them were young people willing to give up their lives for that ideology of Marxism-Leninism and/or for lost lands, or both. Whether the Soviets actually believed what they espoused or not, their means used towards their goal of global domination by force of arms may never be fully agreed upon. The goal itself is open to debate. What this author believes though, is that every man, woman, and child on the earth was threatened by to Cold War, whether it be by a more tactical terrorism, or the ultimate terror of nuclear war. In later volumes I hope to deal with these and other problems of Cold War history.

This book would not be completed without a discussion of terrorism within the United States, or that possibly caused by the United States. Clearly there were home-grown terrorists, some who received outside support, operating in the US during the Cold War. Clearly some US allies overstepped the bounds or propriety in armed conflict, bringing more animosity towards the US.

I owe a debt of gratitude to some folks for helping make my hobby and academic avocation of writing turned career, into a reality. The first is to my family, to whom this book is dedicated. Rodney Ross and the rest of the staff of the National Archives and Records Administration is in line for thanks in his preparing of records for my examination. Two teachers, Dr. Ed Platt and Rick Gross, played a role in gathering the facts needed to put this book together. The staff of the National Security Archive helped much with the first volume of this series and their internet work helped with this volume. The Freedom of Information Act (FOIA) staff, officially Information and Privacy, at the CIA—including Scott Koch, Delores Nelson, and Kathryn I. Dyer—provided documents that without which, this book would not have been possible. Arthur W. Bergeron, Jr. Ph.D. and Edward T. Otto of the US Army War College and associated organizations at Carlisle Barracks are in line for a thank-you as well. They provided documentation under the FOIA that added greatly to this volume. The library staffs at Youngstown State University, Kent State University, and Indiana University of Pennsylvania were also helpful in finding resources along the way. I also want to thank those too many to recognize that in some way helped along the way in putting together *Cold Warfare I* and *Cold Warfare II*. It is my hope the reader finds this volume, created from many sources and with the help of the above, both interesting and informative.

Patrick Pacalo, Ph.D.
Boardman, Ohio, USA, June 2008

Introduction: Why a Book on Cold War Terrorism?

Everyone, or almost everyone, chooses a vocation in life. I chose the profession of arms. It carried me around the country and as far as Germany. 1 went from TOW missile crewman, to tank platoon leader, to intern at the Strategic Studies Institute (SSI). I served in the National Guard and Army Reserve. After the Infantry and Armor jobs I was given the opportunity to serve in the Chemical Corps on an Armor Battalion operations staff. My final assignment was an opportunity that I had coveted to some degree. I served as a reserve intelligence officer in a Chemical Brigade during Desert Storm but never deployed to the Kuwaiti Theater of Operations.

One day I walked into the reserve center a year after passing my Captain' s board, and shortly after being assigned to that post. My "boss," a Major in intelligence, handed me a carousel of 35 mm slides and told me I was going to do a briefing on Sabotage and Espionage Directed Against the Army (SAEDA) in twenty minutes. Pre-9/11 there was a lot to question about what actions we could take and what were out of our jurisdiction. Being out of the military for some time now I cannot say for sure how things run. I can only hope that the ambiguities we had to deal with have been cleared up.

My military experience was for the most part in the "peacetime Army" and I do not seek to compare it with anyone else's experience. Clearly many in uniform had it tougher than anything I did. However, we all learn from our experiences. I am only grateful for the experience I gained and the superb men and women I had the opportunity of serving with.

My civilian job during the Gulf War was on the safety and health staff at Georgetown University, and when I arrived at the unit, I was expected to be some kind of hot-shot by my boss in the Reserve. I think that, on that one, truth was far from the assumption. I do remember an occurrence one early morning at GU, when the SCUD missies were flying and the bombs were dropping in the Gulf, and I was in the office before 8:00 a.m. The phone rang and a meek female voice asked if we needed gas masks. I told her things would be fine and we did not require them. The logistics and public relations nightmare of issuing 20,000 protective masks made such an action prohibitive. So, you see I had two jobs at once but sometimes responsibilities intermingled.

Concerning the story about the SAEDA briefing, I simply did the best I could with what I had. All I could do was put the carousel in the projector and put one slide at a time up in front of the troops and talk about it extemporaneously. In the intelligence section most of my time was taken up reading reports on terrorism from the Foreign Broadcast Information System and working with the operations section on the standard operating procedures for a new computer system. Fortunately, I had great troops and NCOs working with me. Our Brigade (the 464th Chemical) was commanded by a General, and I had never worked so closely with a flag ranked officer. I think I briefed the General on two occasions. I left the service for good, of my own volition and with an honorable discharge in hand, in 1994.

How did I become interested in war and terrorism, and how did I get to where I was in 1991? Why did I become interested enough in the subject to write this book? It started with interest in military history and branched out from there. By virtue of my growing up a as the son of a career military officer during the Vietnam Era, I knew a little about national security at a young age. Later, my own humble Army Guard and Reserve service brought me more knowledge and some experience in strategic studies. I was fortunate enough to have some high school and college teachers along the way who taught about the Cold War and terrorism.

My father, Nicholas Pacalo Sr., born in the town of Campbell, Ohio, in 1933, attained the rank of Navy Captain (Naval Aviator) and was stationed at the Pentagon in the 1970s. In the earlier days, living in places like New Jersey, it was not as intense as it was living on the Virginia side of the Washington D.C. area. Sometimes it was interesting in the earlier days, but not as glamorous as those later days.

Dad was not the first generation in the family to serve in the armed forces. My Romanian-born grandfather had served in the US Army in WWI. He fought in such hellish places as Verdun and suffered a bullet wound and was a surviving toxic gas casualty. In addition, one of my great grandfathers was killed in the Romanian Army in WWI.

"Captain Nick," as my father would be known years later (not to his knowledge) when he retired from the Navy and taught at a university, flew the anti-submarine patrol aircraft known as the P-2 Neptune in the 1950s. The Neptune was a strange bird, with two jets and two propeller engines. It was capable of carrying nuclear munitions such as mines, depth charges, and torpedoes for tracking and if necessary, hunting the Soviet nuclear missile submarines that threatened the USA. As we know, open warfare of this type never happened. This dangerous and adventuresome assignment was undertaken well before I was born in 1963.

In the mid-1960s, we were stationed at McGuire Air Force Base, New Jersey, when my dad was flying the C-130 Hercules in and out of Vietnam. Later, we were stationed at Lakehurst Naval Air Station, New Jersey, when he was flying a variety of aircraft such as the S-2 Tracker aircraft carrier based anti-submarine plane, and training Naval Reserves during the middle and late 1960s. Lakehurst is famous as the site where the huge German airship Hindenburg crashed in 1937. The gargantuan airship hangers are still there to this day.

At Lakehurst, Dad often took us to the base and let us climb around in the fixed wing aircraft and helicopters. On one occasion, while crawling around in a helicopter, I pulled up on a handle with both hands and said, "Hey, Dad, what's this?" An urgent, "No, no, no, don't do that," was the response I got. I had been pulling on the handle that might have retracted the landing gear of the chopper and crashed it to the ground. There was a safety device that was supposed to prevent this. My dad was the safety officer for the base and a standing family joke is that the headline in the local paper might have been "Safety Officer's Son Wrecks $10 Million Helicopter."

During this time my mother's energy was spent raising us kids, three boys (myself; one older brother, Nick Jr.; and one younger brother, Jack) and my younger sister Carla. Life in the military environment was not always easy. Mom added to her responsibilities by working as a Registered Medical Technologist. Later she would change careers to that of an elementary school teacher. Mom came from Youngstown, Ohio, and is of Italian ancestry.

My changing of schools during my dad's various duty assignments was often stressful. We lived in neighborhoods that were heavily populated with military and government personnel. In spite of the stress, it was a learning experience. I met people with interests out of the ordinary and learned much about the wider world around me. I learned positive and negative facts about American and world politics, and history.

My earliest memory of a public event was the first Apollo program moon landing in 1969. Shortly afterwards the story of the My Lai massacre of innocent civilians in Vietnam broke in the news and, in the second grade, my classmates were discussing it on the playground. Three years later in 1972, the Palestinian terrorists killed the Israeli athletes at the infamous Munich Olympics. I was learning that there could be tragic excesses in war, and that terrorism was a horrible thing. I was also beginning to build the separate but related belief that the Cold War, with its terrorism and nuclear mutual assured destruction, threatened all humankind.

In the 1970s, we lived in Annandale, Virginia, part of Northern Virginia, fourteen miles from the Pentagon where my father worked. The neighborhood had the idyllic name of Springbrook Forest and was sufficiently supplied with wooded Fairfax County "parkland" and a stream of significant size. Today we might call this wooded wet area amidst the houses by the more complex name of a "riparian setback." Sufficient to say it was land preserved. The area was rich in the financial sense as well, and both parents were college graduates in many homes, not nearly so common as today.

In the 7th grade I started classes at Lake Braddock, a new multimillion dollar school that served grades 7 through 12 and had approximately 4,000 students. A million dollars was a lot of money in those days, even considering that our parents worked in the hundreds of millions and billions. The school was fully air conditioned, had wall-to-wall carpet, and had few internal walls. Four classes might meet in one large area and students were encouraged to move around and stretch out on the floor. I was elected class treasurer of the 743-person class of 1981, by a clear majority, and had many friends.

One of the acquaintances I made was Larry Nguyen, a recently emigrated Vietnamese boy who spoke excellent English. We traded in the beer can collecting club, that juvenile hobby being quite a rage in the middle 1970s. There was something unusual about Larry, and it had to do with his father. Larry and his family had come to the United States in 1975 when the South Vietnamese capital Saigon fell to the Communist Army from North Vietnam.

Larry's father was the former Saigon Police Chief, General Nguyen Ngoc Loan. He executed the bound Viet Cong prisoner Nguyn Vin Lem in the confines of the city. An infamous photograph was taken of the event by Eddie Adams, an Associated Press photojournalism who eventually covered thirteen wars. Adams won the Pulitzer Prize for the February 1968 photo. The events took place during the Tet Offensive. The event was also filmed by NBC News.

There are other viewpoints on what happened in Saigon in February 1968. Some sources state that Lém commanded a Viet Cong assassination unit which was targeting South Vietnamese police and their families. Other stories of that day state that he was shooting at civilians when he was apprehended. The other side of the coin is that Loan himself was practicing terrorism.

To support his family, Larry's father opened a pizza parlor in a mini-mall not too many miles from Springbrook Forest. It is pretty fair to say that everybody in Northern Virginia knew about the events in Saigon in February of 1968. Some called the restaurant "General Wu' s pizza," though I do not know why it picked up that nickname. I was in the shop several times and met the general at least once. The CBS news magazine *60Minutes* featured the situation and asked whether it was fair to allow the General to live in the US and sell pizza. The pizza was not bad, by the way.

I was learning there was a very dark side to life. While things here in America were very good, in some places in the world they could be very bad. Further, these events around the globe were, or at least could be, interrelated with everyday America.

Other people in Northern Virginia had an impact on my world view during the 1970s. Our next-door neighbor was Ron Underwood; he worked for the United States Information Agency [USI A] and had a son, Clay, who was my age. USI A provided information about America and our form of government and culture to other countries around the world. The agency was sort of goodwill ambassadors who provided the global PR for American democracy. Ron was a good-natured individual and a designer by trade. He was a graduate of Duke University. We had sort of an exchange program going with the Underwoods and other sons and fathers in the neighborhood for a while. Bobby Curran and his father, another US Navy Captain is one that came to mind. Clay Underwood and I rode in with my dad to his office and spend one day at the Pentagon. The three of us met Ron for lunch at Hogates, a fancy Washington restaurant. Several weeks later Clay and I went to Ron' s office and at mid day meet my dad for lunch. Clay and I did not always have friendly relations, there were one or two juvenile fist fights between us in those days.

On one of these occasions at the USIA my picture was taken for an exhibition which was going to South America. I had dark curly locks then and

I was to "represent the Italian-Americans" in a collage of photos of people from the U S, according to Underwood. Clay was blond and fair skinned and he represented the Nordic-Americans. Our pictures toured the South American continent in a show designed by Ron Underwood.

Many of the houses that backed up to the woods, as ours and the Underwoods' did, had decks. I recall one afternoon sitting on the Underwoods' deck, just Ron and me. We were talking about the politics of the Cold War. He said something that stuck with me until long after it proved true. He said, "The Soviet Union is not a country, it is an empire of fourteen separate captive states." I did not know what to make of it until the Soviet Union was successfully broken into fourteen pieces in 1991. It was then that I remembered what Underwood had said. Political education often comes in fits and starts, and we do not always put it to use until it is history. How to defeat communism because of the threat it posed was becoming an obsession with me back then. Fascination with terrorism as apolitical tool came later.

Many of my friends from that era were equally concerned, and though independent of my decision, would follow me when I made the decision to go into the service a few days after my seventeenth birthday. Frank Paty served in a Special Forces unit. John Dyson went to The Citadel and was assigned to the 101st Airborne Division. Brian Roberts went to the 82nd Airborne Division and served in Desert Storm. Bobby Curran joined the Merchant Marine. Ralph Powell went to the regular Army. Gary Cruchfield went to the USMC. Dan Spence and Kevin Park joined the National Guard. Michael Powell, Colin Powell's son, went to Germany as an Army officer. There were others who were also acquaintances and friends.

One last item from Northern Virginia taught me political lessons; this lesson was directly about terrorism and its impact on Springbrook Forest. A family man down the street worked for the US Government Printing Office (GPO); some say he worked for CIA. He was assigned to Beirut and took his family with him. Frank Paty got a letter from one of the man's sons. While watching the *Wonderful World of Disney* on TV, he heard a tremendous explosion down the street. Someone had blown up the grocery store in the neighborhood. The civil war in Beirut was on. Amazing how American culture made it to the four corners of the world.

Things got worse for this family. The father was eventually captured and held hostage for a number of months. For a while it was not even known if he was alive. This was all a number of years before the infamous Iranian hostage crisis. Our neighbor, whoever he worked for, was eventually released alive for better or worse by his captors.

Shortly before I turned sixteen my dad retired from the Navy. He took a college teaching job and we moved to the small college town of Indiana, Pennsylvania. The town had about 15,000 residents, bolstered by about 12,000 students. Arriving in the eleventh grade in 1979, I found that my high school class was less than half the size my class had been at Lake Braddock. I also found that there was a school holiday for the first day of deer season. Clearly this place was different than Northern Virginia. There would be several saving graces to Indiana though, and in the end the place proved beneficial to me and my family.

The first boon at Indiana High School was a teacher named Rick Gross. When I went up to the school to register before classes started, I stated my interest in politics to the counselor and was offered a course called "US and World Affairs." Gross taught the course and instructed in the ideologies of communism, fascism, and capitalism during the first semester. On his desk were the dual flags of the US and the UN. In the second semester he taught such subjects as terrorism. When he taught a subject, he taught it from that viewpoint. He taught communism so well he, without his knowledge, took on the nickname of "Comrade Gross" or just "Comrade."

One day after class he and I were talking about the recent Soviet invasion of Afghanistan. During the class Rick had said there was the possible comparison to our variously available reactions to Afghanistan, and to the Munich agreement of 1938 between Britain and Germany. At Munich the British had allowed Hitler to march into the nation of Czechoslovakia and encouraged him to storm into Poland, which started WWII. Would we now show weakness before the Soviets and if we did would that precipitate W Will? I asked the teacher if he really thought the events compared. He said, "If we do nothing they do." This was all very serious to me.

In a not-so-serious vein I was able to participate in more activities at Indiana High. I was in two plays in the dramatics club, something I never would have done at Lake Braddock. More important was the school started a soccer team my first year there. I was able to play varsity soccer on that first team.

Sparked by patriotism and having nothing better to do, on September 12, 1980, eight days after my seventeenth birthday, I joined the local Infantry Unit of the Pennsylvania Army National Guard. I had my senior year ahead of me and I did not want to quit school to enlist in the regular Army, and did not want to wait till graduation to serve.

I was sworn in to the Guard after school one day in the woodshop of the local unit commander (Captain Nixon), who was a teacher at Indiana High. I signed papers which included answers to dozens, no, pages of, questions such as whether I had ever sued anyone or ever had a homosexual experience. My parents were present and had to sign for me also since I was under eighteen. Before he signed the papers my dad looked at me across the worktable, eyes to eyes, and said "Are you sure you want to do this?" A simple "Yes," was my answer.

In the first four years of service in the Guard and enrollment in the Indiana University of Pennsylvania Reserve Officer Training Corps (ROTC) for two years, I had a diversity of experience. A high school classmate heard about the money to be made in getting a commission in the Guard (I would earn in a commission in three years, at age nineteen, in a special program). It was no trouble recruiting him. I served on a TOW heavy anti-armor missile crew, graduated Airborne School (jump school), completed enlisted basic training, acted as an ROTC Cadet Company Commander, and was commissioned as a Second Lieutenant and tank platoon leader in an Armor unit at age nineteen as the program allowed.

My internship was in residence at the Strategic Studies Institute of the Army War College at Carlisle Barracks, Pennsylvania. My course of study lasted from late August 1983 to the middle of December of the same year. I found much controversial information but was exposed to little about terrorism. I remember one film on terrorism, and significant though it was, it was only one film.

Shortly after my internship a friend, David Freda, a fellow soccer player at Indiana High, was then a student at Carnegie Mellon University. He left for a year of liberal arts study at the university in Bologna, Italy. I called him in the summer of 1984 and he suggested I come over for a visit. I dropped everything and was in Italy in a few days, my first time out of the country. I flew a now long defunct super-budget airline called People Express, famous for $ 149.00 flights to Europe. I flew into Gatwick, London, purchasing a rail pass on arrival and made my way to Bologna, Italy, from there, through much of the continent. The clerk at the airport in London sold me a rail pass intended for European students and it included free travel in Easther (Communist occupied) Europe and North Africa though I did not make use of it for those areas.

Making my way across town to where Dave was living in an apartment was almost as challenging as getting to Bologna had been. There is the truism that, "everyone speaks English in Europe," I found this not to be the case in Italy, Austria, or in the low-countries. I passed one policeman on a Bologna sidewalk who was carrying a sub-machinegun. Clearly this was different than America. The heavy armament was not without cause. I heard later that a few years before the Bologna rail station had been bombed, probably by the Italian Red Brigades or right-wing reactionaries.

We consumed a lot of wine while I was in Bologna. The bars were called osterias and my first night there I was treated to a visit to one of them. After one night of heavy drinking while we watched the previous season' s American Super Bowl with some of the locals we went touring. I had drunk twelve Peroni beers during that night's engagement; we drove my rented car, a sporty primo standard transmission Italian Lancia, up to the American Army base at Vicenza.

Why we drove to the base I do not know. It was my idea. I think I just wanted to see if we could get in on our American passports and my National Guard identification card. Vicenza was the home to the 509th Airborne (Parachute Infantry Regiment). They were part of the elite. The small base was right smack in the middle of the town which was north of Bologna. I am not sure how we found it. Dave handled the map.

We got to the gate and were promptly stopped by a paratrooper. I got out of the car and showed him my military ID and my passport and identified myself as a paratrooper. I asked him if I could gain access to the base and bring my American friend onto the base. He pointed to a second-story window overlooking the place where we stood. He said, "There is an M-60 machinegun in that window trained on us."

The guard then said he would allow us onto the base if I would surrender Dave's American passport to be picked up at the gate when we left. We complied. We had breakfast at the commissary, not much of which I was able to eat from last night's debauch, and shopped briefly at the PX. We then made our way off base having seen, what was for us a tourist attraction, however serious a place it was for those based there.

On the drive back, we took a different route along the Po River. I saw signs of communist influence. They were in the form of markers outside some of the many farms we passed. The farmers had sunk large tractor tires halfway into the ground and painted them white. On these tires they painted the word

"Communista," translated from Italian to simply mean Communist. The region around Bologna was known for being "red."

Sometime after returning to Bologna, I placed a telephone call to the Underwoods [Ron was still working for the USIA, however, was now assigned to Vienna, Austria]. To make this telephone call we had to go down to the phone company in Bologna. I asked if I could come visit them in Vienna for a few days and they said sure. A couple days later and an overnight train ride into Austria and I was at the Vienna train station. The whole Underwood family was living in Vienna. The most gracious Norma, Ron's wife and also a Duke University graduate, and Clay all lived in a beautiful apartment in the quiet outskirts of the city. I did not see Clay on that trip as he was off on summer travel around Europe. Ron and Norma put me up in their spare room.

On my arrival at the station, I called Norma at their home. She said she would have Ron come over from the embassy and pick me up in a few minutes. I waited out in the front of the station and Ron arrived in a large shiny Mercedes Benz. He helped me get my bags into the trunk and we were off to their home. I had noticed he had normal Austrian license plates on the car. I asked him why he did not have diplomatic plates if he was entitled to them. His reply was that "then the 'terroristas' will know who I am."

The next day I found my way across town to where Ron worked. My German was barely passable, but I could read a map and follow the directions Norma had given me. At the embassy I got the red-carpet tour. Ron walked me all over the building, showing me, for instance, that the embassy had its own printing operation. He took me to his office and we talked about his work. He was in charge of putting up shows about America throughout Eastern Europe. He worked behind the Iron Curtain border with international communism but was based out of free Vienna.

The stories he told were political and interesting. For instance, in one communist bloc country the USIA put a display and model of the space shuttle in a street-level window of the American embassy. Native people lined up on the sidewalks by the thousands to walk by and see the mock-up of the craft. This was a public relations disaster for the communists. The communist government required that the Americans take down the display and put it up inside the embassy compound. Ron explained that only a handful of people would come in to see it since their government would get a good look at them entering the embassy.

During our talk Ron pointed to the windows behind his desk. He said he tried to get Lexan for these windows. Lexan is what is known as bullet-proof glass. He was concerned about the possibility of terrorist attacks. He said the embassy turned him down on the proposal because of the expense. They suggested putting bars on the windows. Ron said he did not like that idea of the bars because it would be hard to escape in the event of a fire. Clearly terrorism was a concern on the part of US officials in the middle 1980s and Underwood' s concern intrigued me. This was more than just studies at Indiana High, the university, or in the National Guard Armory in Pennsylvania, which were then seemingly far from "the action."

I spent about four days in Vienna. The Underwoods treated me like royalty. They took me out to a different garden or vineyard restaurant every night and never let me pay. There was not so much wine as in Italy, but there was wine. We talked a lot about politics. Norma warned me that the new head of the USIA, a Mr. Wick, was very political and I should watch what I say around the embassy crowd. Ron told me he was troubled by the message "CIA out" spray painted on the wall near the embassy; working for the USIA, he said this really bothered him.

One evening Norma looked me straight in the eyes and said, "There are things I would go to the barricades for." What I think she meant was that there were ideas in this world worth fighting for. Being a member of the National Guard, with its militia traditions, my attitude towards the remark was "more power to ya."

When I left Vienna, I took another night train ride to Northern Europe. After seeing some art museums, I made my way to some of history's great battlefields that dot the area. I visited Waterloo in Belgium where Britain's Duke of Wellington finally defeated Napoleon in 1815.

I then visited the monument at the Battle of the Bulge. This was the place where the Americans had held off German's last great surprise offensive of WWII in the winter of 1944-45. The cost to the US soldiers in the Battle of the Bulge was horrific.

The National Guard unit to which I was assigned was the 28th Infantry Division. The unit had fought at the Bulge. When I walked into the museum and visitors' center at the first thing I saw, and any other visitor would see, was the 28th Division flag. Shock and surprise hardly explain my feeling when I realized how valued the Division's participation in the battle was. Outside the visitors' center was a huge concrete monument that one could climb to the top of and walk around to view the battlefield. Below that, on the columns supporting the monument, were the unit patches of the American units that fought there.

I was wearing an "Airborne" t-shirt and had short hair. I was fairly recognizable as an American soldier. One other tourist consented to take my picture, with my camera, with me standing next to the 28th Division symbol which was a red keystone. A young man I think to have been a local walked up to me after some pictures were taken. He said in broken English, "You American soldier." 1 said, "Yes." He then said something I will never forget "You Bloody Bucket." And I said, "Yes." The "Bloody Bucket" was the nickname given to the 28th because the symbol of the Division was the red Pennsylvania keystone, and to the locals in the area of the Bulge it looked like a bucket. It was "bloody" because of the horrific casualties the division took and its red color. I had learned that was the nickname of the Division during my first drill with the Infantry back in 1980. That was the extent of the conversation and, over the next couple days, I got on my way to cross the English Channel and to London and home.

Throughout the 1980s my involvement with the military gave some re-enforcement to my interest in this field of study. In 1986, while on temporary duty at Fort McClellan, Alabama, I was part of a terrorism-hostage scenario. I played a terrorist with chemical weapons. The US forces subdued myself and my collaborators and won the exercise. Further duty at Fort McClellan in 1988 reinforced the reality of the terrorist threat. In 1991, during Desert Shield/ Desert Storm, I was an intelligence officer in a reserve Chemical Brigade and was responsible for studying documents on terrorism and conducting briefings on the subject (among others). My civilian job was in safety and health engineering at Georgetown University in DC with my title being "safety specialist."

Thus, I hope that the above explains why I have undertaken this search for connections between the Cold War, communism, and terrorism. In what follows, I have endeavored to use the best sources from the National Archives and Records Administration (NARA), the CIA, the US military, the private National Security Archive, and in addition I have used journalistic and other public works from the periods concerned.

Chapter 1: Defining the Problem - The Landscape of Cold War Terrorism

There were huge holes in the system of information sharing, and in general for reactive action, between and among federal agencies during the Cold War regarding terrorism. This became all too clear after 9/11 and even to state it now may seem a cliche. However, the Cold War gave birth to the system of anti-terrorism and terrorism-counter-action that existed in 2001. The post-Cold War new world order was only a decade old at that time.

Anti-terrorism is primarily good security or prevention measures, terrorism-counter-action is interrupting terrorist acts or other use of force to prevent or preempt the terrorists from doing their dirty work. It was a system of compartmentalization where information was not shared out of fear of impinging on civil rights or trampling on bureaucratic turf. People who had been allied during the Cold War became mortal enemies in a morning's time.

What do we mean when we use the word "terrorism"? One definition of terrorism during the Cold War can be found in a publication entitled *Terrorism/ Counter-Terrorism Training Manual* by Arthur Gerringer, the director of the Institute for Strategic Studies on Terrorism:

> . ..terrorism can be defined as the calculated use of violence.. .to attain goals, which are often political in nature, by intimidation.... Terrorism is a criminal act... intended to influence an audience.[1]

Gerringer also states unequivocally that a number of American terrorists received paramilitary training in Cuba and South America. Terrorists in

Western Europe and the Middle East have received direct communist supported training the Soviet Union and North Korea, among other rogue states, according to Gerringer.

All of these are pro-communist or more specifically pro-Soviet countries. Terrorist operations were often well-executed and this was in no small measure because of their training. They were often carried out by clandestine cells, or groups of small secretive units. The terrorists of the Cold War followed a variety of ideological bents: Trotskyism, Marxism-Leninism, Stalinism and Maoism. There were also anarchists and we could name more varieties of ideological choices of the terrorists. Religion often played a role, and as we have seen would do more so after the Cold War. State sponsored terroristic acts tended to be based upon some form of communism and it varied from locale to locale precisely which ideological "flavor" the terrorists chose for their paradigm.

What were people saying about terrorism during the Cold War? Who were those involved in the debate? What were the Soviets doing? What was US policy? Who was responsible for terrorism that was taking place on a global scale? Some of these questions have yet to be answered. In Congressional testimony one expert had this to say:

> There exists a large communist terroristic force... interwoven with Soviet and anti-Soviet strategies relating to deterrence and initiation of war.
> Stefan Possony, a senior fellow (emeritus) of Stanford University's Hoover Institution, 1981.[2]

As the above demonstrates, there was much available published scholarship and journalistic research on terrorism as a global threat prior to 9/11/01. However, none of this work informed policy makers well enough for America to have avoided 9/11. Perhaps during the Cold War too much attention was focused on terrorist politics and ideology versus their capabilities. The carryover of this outlook might have been a contributor to the success of the attacks by al Qaida in 2001 and thereafter. During the Cold War the oft used pabulum answer to why there was so little terrorism in the USA was at least twofold. Those asking the question were told that the FBI was proficient at penetrating terrorist networks. Another answer given was that it was difficult for terrorist groups to set up a logistical support tail in America.

Marxist theoreticians Karl Marx and Vladimir Lenin wrote extensively about terrorism. This type of warfare was seen by these communists a legitimate means to effect change. Breaking the will of the foe, if necessary, by terrorism, was seen as means to the end of world revolution. To Marx and the Soviets, terrorism was not just a tactical device for causing havoc; it was a strategic tool to be used to further and foment world revolution.

In 1980, CIA analyst Edward Mickolus wrote a history of terrorism containing a chronology of events. In the work, *Transnational Terrorism,*[3] he concentrated his study on the period from 1968 to 1979. He states that during this period there were 342 acts of terrorism involving the US. Many might find this hard to comprehend. Mickolus is not strong on tying the attacks to this or that nation's support. However, many of the involved violent groups, such as the Palestinian Liberation Organization (PLO), and other international terrorist groups, had direct or indirect ties to the Soviet Union. The PLO was a workhorse for the cause of international terrorism, giving aid and support to a network of terrorist groups, sometimes its own splinter groups, and receiving aid from Soviet client states.

Terrorist groups were often tied to the Soviets through third persons in the form of client countries that were supported massively and directly by the Soviets. Sometimes the ties were more direct from the Soviets to the terrorists and sometimes these ties were evidently less strong. This is not to say that all terrorism during the Cold War period was Soviet inspired. Also, some terrorist groups mellowed or even evaporated over time. The PLO was one such organization that has mellowed somewhat. The organization was backing terrorism for many years but then becoming more political and less violent later.

The US Department of State took a somewhat tactful and middle-of-the-road means of explaining the Soviet role on global terrorism in 1986. From a report of that era, one might read:

> The Soviets and various East European states provide arms and training to a broad spectrum of anti-western groups and "national liberation movements," many of whose members commit terrorist acts. Although the Soviet Union and its allies have sold some arms

directly to some groups, mostly Palestinians, most Soviet weapons sold or given to terrorist groups are provided by Third World Soviet clients, such as Libya.[4]

The Soviets did, however, bring terrorists to the Soviet Union for training on a number of occasions. In a 1981 Senate hearing, Stefan Possony, a senior fellow (emeritus) of Stanford University's Hoover Institution, was more pointed when he testified that:

> The contribution of the USSR has been primarily the creation of a vast infrastructure through which the terrorists can be trained, move from place to place, and engage in "combat...."[5]

Somewhat prophetically (for reasons outside of the Cold War conflict), in a 1981 statement before the US Senate, James Billington, Director of the Woodrow Wilson International Center for Scholars, said the following about America's vulnerability to Soviet sponsored terror:

> A second reason why terrorism may grow is simply the technological vulnerability of most modern urbanized civilizations, particularly our own, to the paralyzing effects of violence....[6]

The CIA weighed in on the matter on a number of occasions. In a 1986 National Intelligence Estimate (NIE) the agency stated:

> The Soviet leaders' approach to terrorism derives from their broader view that violence is a basic, legitimate tool of political struggle to be applied or sponsored in those settings where its use will benefit the USSR. As a result, the Soviets have no moral compunctions about supporting foreign insurgent and terrorist groups, the primary consideration is whether the activities of these groups further Soviet interests.[7]

The CIA's National Foreign Assessment Center had already drawn some conclusions in 1981, just as Ronald Reagan was assuming the office of President. A document entitled "The Supporters of International Terrorism" illustrated how the network of support for terrorism functioned. As stated in the book *Cold Warfare: A Compact History,* by this author, just because the CIA said it, does not make it true. However, this is one official view of Cold War terrorism:

The argument that the Soviets put forth about not supporting international terrorism is a semantic one. It is true that there is no evidence that the Soviets have directly instigated or carried out acts of international terrorism in recent years. It is also true, however, that without indirect Soviet assistance many terrorist groups would find their operations severely hampered. The major go-betweens in the Soviet-terrorism connection are:

Libya
Cuba
South Yemen
Syria
various Palestinian groups[8]

The document traced this indirect support for terror on the part of the Soviets down a level. The document states that groups benefitting from Libyan support included the Provisional Irish Republican Army, all major Palestinian groups, the Baader-Meinhof Gang/Red Army Faction, various Latin American terrorist groups, and Carlos (the Jackal). Further the document states that:

Soviet weapons and Libyan and Syrian support have been funneled
through the Palestinians at least to the following groups:
PIRA(Provisional Irish Republican Army)
Dutch Red Resistance Front
Baader-Meinhof Gang/Red Army Faction
Basque ETA
Armenian terrorists
various Turkish terrorists
most Latin American terrorist groups
Iranian terrorists in the pre-revolutionary period
Japanese Red Army[9]

Throughout the Cold War, and this book concerns terrorism as related to the Cold War, a terrorist in one's view was a freedom-fighter in another's. In the communist nation of Yugoslavia, the Minister of Foreign Affairs, Bosniak Dizarevic, was cited by the Yugoslav news agency Tanjug as saying, "It is wrong to equate liberation struggles and struggles against aggression and racism with terrorism." Dizarevic was speaking to US Secretary of State George Shultz in 1986, while Cold War flames still burned bright.[10] Dizarevic may have been simply puffing the ideological angle, knowing full well that terrorism was a form of warfare against the West, more than it was intended to serve the causes of the divergent groups in existence.

In another look at the question of who is a terrorist, during the 1980s, the US Army Chemical School was teaching that federal soldiers handed out blankets infected with small pox to some Native Americans during the Indian Wars. We can ask, was this terrorism? Throughout history terror has been used by governments to eliminate groups viewed as "socially dangerous." Somewhat conversely, terrorist activity is also a poor person's method of waging war against states perceived as more powerful.

Some might think that the terrorist' s defining goal is to kill as many people as possible in an act or acts of violence. This is a possible definition, but, a better one comes from the name itself, *terrorist*. A terrorist wants, above all, to cause horror, alarm, anxiety, and panic.[11] The terrorist's target is public opinion or more explicitly the mind of the populace, as much as it is innocent people. The violent actor wants the target to believe those targeted are helpless and their government cannot help them. Geography was not a determining factor for terrorists during the Cold War. If attacking targets in a less built-up area achieved the goal of undermining a government, the terrorist did it. If "hitting" a major urban center achieved the goal, the terrorists did that. Terrorism was (is) used to compel, and to the terrorists of the Cold War period there were no innocents anywhere.

Terrorism knows few limits in terms of its impact throughout history. The Jewish Zealots of the first century A.D. have been labeled as terrorists by some. The Zealots killed those they believed to be evil. In the eleventh century, there existed an Iran and Mediterranean-based terrorist group known as the Hashashini. These assassins smoked hashish and spread terror as far as India, introducing martyrdom because they often died in their attacks. Terrorism is nothing new and it surely had a significant impact on the course of the Cold War, many centuries after these two early examples.

During the Cold War, terrorists and terrorist groups tended to group together and formed interconnected networks. This was also true of the nations that supported them. These supporting nations were often interconnected, but sometimes were at odds. So, there was a composite network of working terrorist groups and of supporting nations. Often, they came together as a matter of practical logistics. Just as often terrorist groups and nations came together out of shared ideological beliefs. It could be said, in this case, that "misery loves company" as none of the terrorists, nor any of the nations involved, were at the apex of world development and political power. Certainly, some terrorists hailed from countries such as the Federal Republic of Germany (FRG) and France, but those individuals were not near the top of the power pyramid. The Soviet Union was itself a Cold War superpower but it was a second-class one. The USSR was often referred to as "third world nation with nuclear weapons."

Terrorists could be revolutionaries or insurgents, that is to say they could be actors on an ideological plane or perhaps on a military one. Regardless of motivation, news media coverage was important to the terrorists of the Cold War; publicity helped to spread fear and garner support at the same time. Terrorist acts included, but were not limited to: assassinations, bombings, hostage-taking, kidnaping, military-style raids, seizure of buildings or objects, sabotage, hoaxes, arson, and perhaps most significantly hijackings (usually involving airliners, but in at least one case involving a cruise ship). These groups were anything but docile and passive.

In trying to answer the "why" of Cold War terrorism we can ask, were the groups involved made up of the crazy and thrill seekers? Certainly, all were criminals because terrorist acts require the commission of a crime. Ideology was a driving force behind the nations involved in the Cold War; was it a driving force behind the terrorists? In 1982 author Neil C. Livingstone wrote, "The leadership of terrorist groups is always more ideological than the rank-and-file." Livingstone continued, however:

> ...the leadership and rank-and-file have received political and
> military training in the USSR, Cuba, and the Warsaw Pact nations.[12]

Operating budgets for terrorist groups were another matter entirely. Since the Soviets were perpetually short of hard currency and their own economy was a mess, other sources of funds had to be sought by the terrorists. Therefore, during its more violent days, the Cold War era PLO sought out oil-rich Arab countries, including Saudi Arabia, as benefactors. Reportedly the Saudis urged the PLO leadership to jettison its most Marxists elements such as the Popular Front for the Liberation of Palestine (PFLP). The PLO did not take that advice at that time. Budgets for these groups ran into the hundreds of millions of dollars.[13]

Through the influence of their material support for terrorist groups the Soviets were able to move many of them towards the Marxist left. Some groups like the Red Brigades, active in German, Italy, and Japan, were dedicated Marxist-Leninists from their beginnings. Groups influenced by the Soviet's ideology included the Irish Republican Army (IRA) Provisional wing, the Basque Homeland and Liberty Movement (ETA), the Tupamaros of Uruguay, M-19 of Columbia, and others. M-19 was so violently inclined and anarchistic that it participated in a raid on Colombia's Supreme Court killing a number of the judges. Far from planning and directing each attack by each group, the Soviets preferred to remain significant actors, but to do so in the shadows and to provide material support (such as weapons). The USSR also gave propagandistic support to the terrorists.

The Soviets were not alone at leading major terrorist action during the Cold War. China was also involved. Chinese communism, like Soviet communism, was expansionist given the opportunity. From the *Congressional Record* one might read that:

> In 1965, the Maoists attempted to seize Indonesia. The adventure culminated in an enormous bloodbath of the Indonesian military, who reciprocated against the communists. Terrorism was employed in order to create a mass revolution. The attempt failed and backfired against the Mao regime.[14]

The use of weapons of mass destruction [WMD] and the fear of their use, which during the Cold War were usually referred to in the US as NBC weapons (for Nuclear, Biological, and Chemical), was a possibility during the Cold War. While they themselves had provided such weapons to third parties who used them, the Soviets might actually have served to moderate the actions of terror groups that received direct or indirect support from them. On several occasions the Soviets did use chemical and biological weapons to assassinate individuals who had defected from communism. According to a late Cold War Army manual on the subject of terrorism:

> Fear of alienation by peer and support populations has probably inhibited the use of chemical and biological weapons to date, but this obstacle could evaporate as the competition for headlines increases and public opinion softens.[15]

Cold War terrorists sometimes had elaborate command, control, and communications networks. These networks were the subject of much study in the west, in particular by the US Army. It is evident from the products of these works that much of the theory behind Army doctrine of the 1980s was at least loosely based upon experience with the Viet Cong and on the study of Maoist political ideology. Terrorism was viewed as a tool, requiring a criminal act, to be used primarily in "low intensity" conflict, or wars short of all-out war. The Deputy Chief of Staff for Operations [DCSOPS], headquartered in the Pentagon, was responsible for coordinating the Army's counter-terrorism programs.

Antiterrorism and counterterrorism were the two terms used by the Army to describe its efforts to defeat the terrorists. Antiterrorism was seen as primarily defensive. On the subject of antiterrorism on US soil, the Army said directly that, "Collecting and processing domestic terrorist information is an FBI responsibility."[16] Over half a dozen departments and agencies shared responsibility for antiterrorism with the Army, and it was not the lead agency.

Counterterrorism was "the only reactive phase" involved in plans to stop the terrorists, specifically should they attempt attacks in the US and generally in response to terrorist acts on a global basis. Counterterrorism meant killing terrorists or otherwise resolving situations through the use of force. While antiterrorism meant good security, counterterrorism meant active measures and operations. Military counter-terror forces such as "Delta Force" and the 160th Regiment were created for this purpose. Use of US military forces in domestic terrorism scenarios was a touchy subject. Under protocols developed during the Cold War the Department of Defense [DOD] would only send "observers" initially but might eventually provide operational forces as a situation developed.

Terrorist threat conditions A through D [Alpha through Delta] were delineated in Army doctrine and they are still in use today in a modified form in the Global War on Terror [GWOT]. Each security level became progressively more serious with level Delta being measures aimed at preparation for combat with the terrorists. Lists of procedures for each threat level were developed and published. This was the state of development of Army policy on terrorism during the late Cold War. Many of the measures outlined were shared to some extent with other military organizations and with civilian agencies.

Killing by terrorist groups in transnational venues was not the only means of terrorism during the Cold War. There was also purely political terrorism bent on keeping the Soviets and their revolutionary brethren in power. This very overt and brutal action, taken on the part of governments, most notably the Soviet Union with its strong Marxist-Leninist ideology, killed millions of people. This type of directly government-sponsored action was terrorism; the actions were not undertaken with the goal of leading populations to distrust their governments, but to gain submission of the populace to the extant totalitarian governments in power. Ideology, most significantly in these cases, drove the killing. Those people being "contaminated" by Western ideas were often the first to be targeted for elimination or internment in "reeducation" camps.

Next we will look at the nature of the early Soviet state and its use of terror through the 1950s. It could be argued that the Cold War, in fact, began in 1917-1918 when Lenin launched the red terror on the Soviet people. U S President Woodrow Wilson countered the red terror with a global effort to isolate the Soviets until they stopped the persecution and execution of innocent people.

Chapter 2: Soviet State Directed Terrorism - The First 30 Years of Soviet Power

Prior to the reign of the communists in the Russian Empire, while revolution was beginning to foment, a Russian intellectual named Stepniak wrote:

> An emperor who shuts himself up in prison from fear of terrorism is certainly not a figure to inspire admiration.[17]

Karl Marx (1918-1883) is the ideological father of the USSR. He was much as George Washington was the father of the USA. The difference is that Marx and those that took power and created the Soviet Union had the stated belief in the use of terrorism. Marx proposed a program that was put into action by Vladimir Lenin (1870-1924). "Violence itself is an economic power," said Marx in 1867.[18]

In May of 1849 Marx had already written, "When our turn comes we will not excuse terrorism."[19] Marx's meaning? The communists would practice terror once in power; they would give no excuses. While in later times terrorism would become diffuse with activity spread between many global and loosely linked groups; from the beginning of their state the Soviets constructed a killing machine out of their government. This was their less sophisticated brand of terrorism.

Lenin added to Marx's position that terrorism could be part of a wide political and/or revolutionary war. Lenin advocated terrorism as needing to be part of a comprehensive plan for uprising or other revolutionary undertaking. Terrorism, in Lenin's mind, could supplant but not replace conventional military actions. Through murderous tactics such as forced starvation Lenin's terrorism killed perhaps three million people in the Soviet state.

Once in power Lenin held show trials in order to terrorize opponents and potential opponents internal to the Soviet Union. One set of trials was held in 1922, after most of the fighting in the Soviet civil war was over. As previously stated, the purpose of the show trials was to modify behavior, to terrorize the population into line, not to kill off opponents, nor even to achieve justice. This is a thread that connects early Cold War terrorism with late Cold War terrorism. Some people, called socialist revolutionaries, were simply not "Bolshevik" enough for Lenin. In 1982 Marc Jansen wrote:

> Lenin was not concerned that these trials should exercise justice....
> The trials in question, he considered, should serve the [cause of]
> repression and propaganda.[20]

If there was a "hero" of the Soviet civil war it was Leon Trotsky (1879-1940). During this conflict that gave birth to the USSR, Trotsky raised a victorious five-million-man Red Army. He had great influence in the USSR's leadership until after Lenin's death when Stalin forced him to flee to Mexico. Stalin's terror consumed him as he was assassinated in 1940. Trotsky believed that[64]*intimidation* is a powerful weapon of policy...used to break the will of the foe."[21] Trotsky wrote more explicitly that:

> The law should not abolish terror: to promise that would be self
> delusion or deception: it should be substantiated and legalized in
> principle...only [the] revolutionary consciousness of justice and
> revolutionary conscience can determine the conditions of its
> application in practice.[22]

Trotsky both compared terrorism with conventional war and stated the application of red terror as justified where "white terror" was not. In speaking of white terror, he was pointing the finger at the White Russians who opposed the reds. In *Terrorism and Communism,* he continued:

> The revolution works in the same way: it kills individuals, and
> intimidates thousands. In this sense red terror is not distinguished

from armed insurrection, the direct continuation of which it represents. The state of revolutionary class can be condemned "morally" only by a man who, as a principle, rejects (in words) every form of violence whatsoever consequently, every war and every rising. For this, one has to be morally and simply a hypothetical Quaker.

... We relied on this fact that the proletariat is the historically rising class.... Without red terror, the Russian bourgeoisie, together with the world bourgeoisie, would throttle us long before the coming of this revolution to Europe. One must be blind not to see this, or a swindler to deny it.[23]

The Soviets proved they were internationalists from the early days of their revolution. In 1918 they attempted to install a Soviet system in Finland. The attempt was unsuccessful. They tried later in Hungary with only very limited success.

So how many deaths did it take to terrorize the Soviet populace into nationhood? Lenin had approximately three million individuals executed by the secret police (Cheka), beginning in July of 1918. This dictatorial mass-murder was prior to an unsuccessful attempt to assassinate Lenin. The first Soviet leader also instituted a policy of forcibly starving his opponents to death. Trotsky never got his chance to lead the Soviet state, but doubtlessly he had many killed as he ran the army during the revolution. Stalin is credited with as many as twenty million deaths. Stalin's successor, Nikita Khrushchev, usually seen as a harmless Cold War "clown," is noted to have killed many (perhaps 400,000 people) when he ran the Ukraine under Stalin. Khrushchev's political nickname was "the Hangman of the Ukraine." Many of these executions ordered by Khrushchev were political killings intended to keep the Ukrainians from breaking away from the Soviet Union.[24] The world had never seen this level of terrorism as under these four individuals.

What is the significance of the writings and actions of Marx, Lenin, Trotsky, Stalin, and Khrushchev? These men were the ideological and moral founding fathers of the USSR. They all advocated and practiced terrorism. They were as important to the Soviet state as the legacy of Locke, Washington, Jefferson, and Madison were (are) to the United States. Recognizing the foundation of the USSR as being on the ideals of terrorism in one form or another, if we can call them ideals, Soviet actions throughout the remainder of the Cold War are easier to understand. They supported, directly and indirectly, global terrorism because they believed their cause was just and any means to achieve their goals were acceptable.

In the early days of the Soviet state's existence there was what became known as a "red scare" in the United States. Fear of communist ideology played a significant role in the scare. There were a few bombings, some speechifying, and organizing. The whole affair did not amount to much and some non-US citizens were deported back to their home countries for communist, anarchist, and terrorist activities. Regardless of whether this terrorism was directed from Moscow, it was a resounding flop. It would have fit with Soviet ideology to make such an attempt to subvert America, however short of resources the Soviet state was during the 1920s when the scare occurred. During this time President Wilson was accused of being soft on Bolshevik doctrines for not taking stronger action.

International Soviet terrorism, or attempts at such, certainly did not end in the WWI period. Little remembered today were the abductions of approximately 600 individuals from the West shortly after World War II. These individuals were drugged or duped by East Bloc agents then spirited to the East. Many of the victims were physically overpowered and beaten severely to subdue them.[25] Some captives were held for various periods of time and released. Some died in Soviet labor camps. Abductions occurred through at least 1956. These events occurred before the Berlin Wall was constructed and when the border between East and West was more open than it was in the later days of the Cold War. The information was provided in Congressional testimony by Theodor Hans, a German immigrant and former US Army counter intelligence agent in the US Army.

> Murder by Soviet agents to eliminate foes, knowledgeable defectors, former Communists who left the party to fight communism from the west, and any other opposition considered too dangerous, is well known as one method of gaining political ends.[26]

As he concluded his testimony Hans said:

> ... Soviet actions two years after World War II in…strengthening East German armed forces and security organizations, were never officially publicized nor strongly protested by the US government.[27]

Later, after WWII he served as a civilian working in counter-espionage for the US in West Germany until 1951. Many of the East's targets were easy prey forthe Soviets and their proxies. This was all part of "the running battle of the Cold War," according to Hans. "Many sources and investigators for the US forces and US Information Agency, USIA, were directly endangered by these practices," said Hans.[28] This activity is a classic example of state-directed terrorism.

Korea was an early flashpoint in the Cold War, however, in different respects than Germany. It is well-known that open fighting between the communist North Koreans and the fledgling democracy of the South began on June 25, 1951. However, tension had been brewing there for some years before the invasion. The leftists within South Korea were supported and sometimes led by communists from the North. The following describes the situation between the leftists and the South Korean police in 1948:

> When the left resorted to terrorism to achieve its ends, one of its first targets was the South Korean police force, a logical target for two reasons:(1) there was a reservoir of popular resentment against the police which could be tapped at any time, and (2) it represented the constituted authority which the left was under orders to undermine. The latent popular resentment against the police was a necessary result of the only tradition which the police had to draw upon in execution of their tasks. Whatever administrative skills the police force possessed it learned from the Japanese, at the same time that it was acquiring whatever respect for civil liberties it now possesses. Hence, the police force, faced with the emergency of leftist terrorism, replied in the only way it knew by being ruthlessly brutal in suppressing the disorder.[29]

The Soviets had muscle they could flex directly in respect to the situation. Most of the South's electrical power was coming from the Soviet controlled North. According to the CIA:

> By inciting unrest in South Korea and by choking off the supply of power, the USSR has the capability of effectively sabotaging and delaying any recovery program initiated by the South....The new government [in the South] will also have to contend with a continuous effort on the part of the communist "fifth column" to instigate sabotage and disorder on the basis of economic and political discontent, thus multiplying the difficulties now existing.[30]

Simultaneous with these activities were the communist takeovers inspired by the Soviets throughout Eastern Europe. The Soviets were using subterfuge and terrorism to do what they knew they could not achieve by conventional war. This is in large part due to the fact that in 1948 the US possessed nuclear weapons and the Soviets did not. A large-scale Soviet conventional invasion of countries around its periphery would probably have met a US nuclear response.

One terrorist attack that seems to have little to do with the Soviets, bears some mention here. President Harry Truman, a National Guard Artillery Captain in WWI, was attacked on November 1, 1950, by Puerto Rican nationalists. While the President was in Blair House in Washington, D.C., two armed members of the liberation front rushed the house. The President's bodyguards opened fire. One bodyguard was killed and one attacker was killed in the melee. Two bodyguards and the other attacker were wounded.

The President said little about the attack in the days that followed. In a November 2 news conference he said, "There's no story so far as I am concerned. I was never in danger. The thing I hate about it is the fact that these young men—one of them killed, and two of them badly wounded. It's all so unnecessary for a thing like that to happen."

Thus, we see that the Soviets were inspired to use terror to spread ideology from its inception in 1917-1918. We can also see that there were serious terrorist attacks that seemingly had little to do with the Cold War. This Soviet-backed activity continued throughout the time period leading up to the Korean War; however, there were many fits and starts to Soviet policy and actions.

After the Korean War the Soviets entered a new and even more global phase in supporting terrorism. Rather than direct but covert action, such as the abductions in Germany immediately following WWII, they supported with material and training many anti-democratic groups around the world. The Soviets were building an empire based upon terrorism; in fact they had already built one by the time they coaxed the North Koreans to invade the South in 1950. In the following chapters some of the groups and methods of Soviet support for the terrorism that followed the Korean War will be examined.

Chapter 3: Middle Eastern Terrorist Groups and Their Supporters - Terror Brokers or Freedom Fighters?

In May 1964, several hundred representatives met at the Intercontinental Hotel in East Jerusalem and founded the Palestine Liberation Organization or PLO as it is commonly known. "Their purpose was to destroy the state of Israel and replace it with an Arab state called Palestine."[31] The organization did not become an actor on the world stage overnight, but the Soviets were not far behind in bringing aid to a group they hoped would disrupt the West "The urban guerrilla concept surfaced in 1968. During the same year the Soviets initiated their extensive help to the PLO."[32]

According to testimony before the sub-committee on terrorism of the Senate Judiciary Committee:

> In 1968 we also witnessed the beginnings of the Baader-Meinhof gang. Their first action: arson in a department store in Frankfurt. In 1972, there occurred the massacre [of 11 Israeli athletes] by the PLO at the Munich Olympiad. Subsequently the PLO attacked the OPEC oil ministers at Vienna.[33]

> The turbulent events of the 1960s culminated in a decision by the Politbureau of the CPSU to develop international terrorism as a major strategic program."[34]

As stated above, terrorism was clearly not a new phenomenon in the 1960s. However, some in the West saw it as a legitimate form of struggle against so called "institutional terror" practiced by countries like the United States. This institutional terrorism supposedly underlay the terrorism practiced by the PLO and other Arab groups which spun off from the PLO, such as the infamous Abu Nidal faction. The terrorism practiced by these groups was nothing more than a "form of protest" in this view.[35] In Nidal's view terrorism is the have-nots against the haves or the poor against the rich.

Abu Nidal, whose real name is Sabri al-Banna, was sixty-five years old when he reportedly shot himself while living in Bagdad in August 2002. Nidal and the operations perpetrated by his organization were responsible for the deaths of hundreds of terrorism victims over the years since the 1970s. As the head of the Fatah—the Revolutionary Council group, Nidal broke with the Palestine Liberation Organization in 1974, saying the organization and Yasser Arafat were too moderate. "Abu Nidal is a craven and despicable terrorist, and the world would certainly be a better place without people like Abu Nidal," Deputy US State Department spokesman Philip Reeker told reporters.

Reeker said the fact Nidal apparently died in Iraq was further proof of Iraq's support of terrorism. "Iraq's record of providing support, safe haven, training, logistical assistance and financial aid to terrorist groups like the Abu Nidal organization is why Iraq is listed as a state supporter of terrorism," he said.[36]

Nidal was prolific in his terrorism. He launched some ninety attacks and killed approximately 300 people. Another 600 were wounded. Most famous of his "work" was the Rome and Vienna airport attacks on December 27, 1985. Sixteen people were killed and ninety-nine wounded when Nidal's terrorists opened fire inside the airports with grenades and automatic weapons.

In a 1986 interview with the German magazine *Der Spiegel,* Nidall shed some light on his overt motivations for his actions. Nidal is known to have gotten support from the USSR. According to Nidal:

> If there is anything absolute in this world, it is our enmity against American imperialism. Without American help, the Zionist state [Israel] would not still exist.[37]

Noting the alleged consequences over his split with the PLO in the 1970s he said, "Arafat's people have tried many times to kill me."[38] As an aside Nidal is said to have made attempts on Arafat's life on numerous occasions.

Former US Ambassador to the United Nations [1981-1985] Jeane Kirkpatrick had this to say on the subject of the PLO and its off-shoots as justified liberators:

> ...all utilize violence, all are closely tied to the Soviet Union and all actively support Soviet policies in Afghanistan, Angola, Nicaragua, and around the world...[39]

By the late 1970s some 7,000 PLO terrorists had been trained in the Soviet Union. During the Cold War, Soviet and terrorist interests were parallel, that is to say they both had no love lost for America. The Soviets hated the US for its strength and democratic ideology. The Middle Eastern terrorists hated America because of its support for Israel. They also tended to be antidemocratic. The Soviets were using the terrorists as surrogates to perform disreputable tasks, at the same time this allowed the Soviets to keep their distance from the acts of terror.[40] It was no coincidence that the terrorists often used Soviet and East Bloc weaponry and logistical support.

One other PLO spin-off was the Palestine Liberation Front (PLF), which was run by one Abu Abbas. He first left the PLO for the Marxist Popular Front for the Liberation of Palestine (PFLP). Unhappy there he created the PLF. Even though he split with the PLO he continued to receive support from that organization and thus was an indirect client of the Soviets. In 1985, Abbas captured the cruise ship *Achille Lauro* and executed Leon Klinghoffer, a wheelchair-bound American citizen. This act was in addition to numerous other terrorist attacks on the part of the PLF. On April 15, 2003, Abbas was captured in Baghdad by American Special Forces. He died of natural causes while in American custody on March 8, 2004.

The most stunning act of terrorism of its time was the seizure of the Israeli athletic team at the 1972 Munich, Germany, Olympics. The group that conducted the attack called themselves "Black September." They took this name because the Jordanian government, which had been giving the PLO sanctuary, used force to remove them from Jordanian soil. The expulsion from Jordan took place in September 1970; hence the name Black September.

The attack on the athletes' quarters took place on September 5 and by September 6, eleven athletes were dead. All of the terrorists were killed or captured. The terrorists had gotten exactly what they wanted; the events of those two days were seen on TV around the world. The coverage included a climactic night gun battle at the airport as the terrorists tried to make their way out of Germany with the hostages. President Nixon said of the events, "We are dealing here with international outlaws of the worst sort who will stoop to anything in order to accomplish their goals, and who are totally unpredictable."[41]

Terrorism was not an oft-used word prior to Munich. After Munich it was forever in the vernacular. The US government was not totally unconcerned though. Hijackings in the Middle East, and some unrelated to that area in the US, were the cause of new policies to be written by the FAA. From Nixon's papers we read:

> These regulations mandate immediate steps by every [commercial air] carrier to prevent or deter the carriage of weapons or explosives aboard its aircraft, to prevent or deter unauthorized access to its aircraft, to tighten its baggage check-in procedures, and to improve the security of its cargo and baggage loading operations.[42]

On September 25, 1972, only a relative few days after Munich, Nixon acted to establish a cabinet committee to combat terrorism. The committee was established, however, there is little historical evidence that the committee accomplished anything. Nixon's memorandum on the subject said in part:

> Because of the great importance and urgency I attach to dealing with the worldwide problem of terrorism, which encompasses diplomatic, intelligence, and law enforcement functions, I am hereby establishing a cabinet committee to combat terrorism.[43]

One week later Nixon signed the "Convention for the Suppression of Unlawful Acts Against the Safety of Civil Aviation." This document had the status of being an international treaty. Nixon said it would "help combat terrorism around the world." There were many hijackings during the remainder of the Cold War and it seems this agreement was ineffectual and barely worth the paper it was printed on.

In small increments the terrorists were getting what they wanted. They were forcing Americans to take notice of their cause, and they were causing inconvenience. In a memo three weeks after Munich, Nixon formed a special cabinet committee to combat terrorism. It was ordered that, "Federal officers and Federal departments and agencies are to cooperate fully with the cabinet committee." This was the first US presidential action clearly targeted at protecting America from global terrorism. The document also stated that, "The Secretary of State will be in touch with other governments and international organizations toward this goal."[44]

A few days after the Jordanian ousting of the PLO from its territory, some support came from around the globe. At that time the Chinese Communists issued one of a number of statements in support of the PLO. There is evidence that the Chinese gave actual material and training support as well as ideological and propagandistic support to the PLO. The statement called the Israelis "lackey" Zionists under the thumb of "US imperialism." More specifically the statement of September 21, 1970, said in part:

> The Palestinian people's revolutionary struggle is a just cause enjoying abundant support. We believe that so long as the Palestinian and other Arab people persist in unity, persevere in armed struggle, fear no threat and refuse to be deceived, they will certainly frustrate all military attacks and political schemes of US imperialism.... The Palestinian and other Arab peoples are sure to win! US imperialism and its collaborator and lackeys are bound to be defeated."[45]

As for what we know now, that could not necessarily be proved absolutely during the Cold War, Soviet support of Palestinian terror groups is all but obvious. According to two researchers who have examined Soviet archives there were high level contacts between Moscow and PLO splinter groups and the PLO itself:

KGB files shed light on the clandestine cooperation between Soviet intelligence and the PFLP. They show the KGB maintained close contacts with leftist Palestinian terrorists.[46]

Probably not coincidentally, the PLO sought peace some two years after the Soviet Union broke up and the Cold War ended. The PLO's life water had dried up. While other terror organizations with other sponsors would step in to fill the void, the PLO was at least overtly seeking a truce. According to author Barry Rubin:

> Yasir Arafat's moment of victory and moment of surrender were one and the same, as he shook hands with Israeli Prime Minister Yitzhak Rabin on September 13, 1993, standing on the White House lawn....[47]

Chapter 4: The Mess in Cambodia

Terror, sponsored by states against their own people was not limited to the Soviet Union as outlined above. In the Cambodia of the 1970s millions were killed by communist elements within the country. Forced emptying of the country's cities, mass executions, and starvation were the mechanisms of murder in Cambodia.

Cambodia, or Kampuchea as it was known for a short time during the Cold War, was entangled in that conflict for at least twenty years. The Khmer people of the area of what is modern Cambodia have an ancient culture. Geographically, the country lies among the borders of Thailand, Laos, and Vietnam. The capital of Phnom Pen is located in the south-central portion of the country.

Cambodian involvement in the Cold War was brought about as a result of the war between North and South Vietnam and their sponsors. According to the CIA:

> The Viet Cong employed Cambodia more and more as the war went on. They used it as a refuge, a depot, and a messenger route. The first Viet Cong base area formed inside Cambodia in early 1960.[48]

After some fifteen years of being entangled in the Vietnam conflict the government of Cambodia collapsed and the Khmer Rouge entered Phnom Pen. The Khmer Rouge was the strongest Cambodian Communist force at the time. From 1975 when the cities were emptied by the Khmer Rouge, until 1979 when the Vietnamese took over the nation, Cambodia was one large labor camp. Trials were dispensed with and individuals, who in any way appeared intellectual, such as by wearing glasses, were executed. Those guilty of petty offenses were also summarily executed.

Approximately two million Cambodians were killed in this time. Pol Pot, one of the most notorious communist dictators of all time, was responsible for the killings. As with many communist leaders of the past he changed his name to affect his Marxist persona. He was born Saloth Sar in 1925. He was exposed to communism while studying in France and died in the jungle in 1998. Pol Pot sought to eliminate not only the ideologically unfit, but the tribes of peoples he believed were alien to Cambodia.

Included in the timeline of Cambodia's modern history are events before and after the establishment of communist Viet Cong bases in the country. From 1946 to 1953 various Cambodian groups resisted French colonial occupation. In 1969, the US bombed Viet Cong bases and supply lines, with the approval of the Cambodian government. In 1975 the cities were emptied by the Khmer Rouge; from 1979 to 1989 the Vietnamese occupied Cambodia; in 1997 Pol Pot was placed under house arrest; and in 1998 Pol Pot died and the Khmer Rouge disbanded.

During Pol Pot's reign, approximately four million people were removed from the cities and villages and relocated into the countryside. This was government-directed terrorism based on an ideology that stated peasant life was superior to city life. Written materials, such as rare manuscripts, were destroyed. Government workers were uprooted with the rest of the population or were outright killed. All this began on April 17, 1975. In Pol Pot's Khmer Rouge enforced marches from city to countryside, over a quarter-million souls perished.

A document released to the public in February 1987 seems to demonstrate some little-known facts about the early history of the Communist takeover in Cambodia. The major thrust of the information contained in the report shows that the Vietnamese military and political fronts were involved in pushing for a takeover of the country prior to the end of US involvement in the war in 1973. Dated May 1972, the report states in part:

> The most convincing evidence of Vietnamese involvement in the rebellion continued to be the movement and training of people. According to a recent defector's report, additional Cambodian tribesmen—including Jarai, Rhade, and Bahnar—marched off to

North Vietnam for training in June 1968. A year later, "Khmer Rouge" battalions were reported on the way to training centers in Attopeu Province in Southern Laos. A recent Vietnamese rallier said he saw a group of Cambodians entering the northeast in August 1969. Armed with pistols and automatic rifles, they said they had just finished "studying in North Vietnam."[49]

The document continues:

The Vietnamese Communists know what they are working with in Cambodia, and have adjusted accordingly. Vietnamese soldiers still do most of the serious fighting—as they do in Laos—and the Khmer Liberation Army, like the Pathet Lao, plays a secondary role.[50]

As Lenin had his secret police, or Cheka, in 1917, the communists had their Khmer secret police in due time prior to the communist take over of that country. "The security apparatus maintains the interrogation facilities and 'thought reform' camps traditionally found in communist territories,"[51] says the intelligence report of 1972. Finally, another close comparison is drawn between the Cambodian communists and the oldline communist governments, "...the Cambodian Party fits the standard mold. It has committees, chapters, and cells with admission procedures like those in Vietnam and the Soviet Union. One report even claims the party flag displays a hammer and sickle."[52]

Under the Khmer Rouge the country was renamed Democratic Kâmp chéa. This is not unusual for communist states during the Cold War, many of them had "democratic" or "republic" in their name. These states were democratic republics in name only.

In 1979, the Khmer Rouge government was overthrown by forces from Vietnam and Cambodia. A less despotic socialist state was established at that point. In 1989, socialism was completely abandoned by Cambodia. In 1993, a new constitution restored ancient the monarchy in the country.

The terror of chemical and biological weapons use was a problem that reared its ugly head in Cambodia, as well as neighboring Laos, and also in Afghanistan. Investigation by the US Department of State and the Arms Control and Disarmament Agency under Ronald Reagan tended to prove that the Soviets were guilty of supplying or using these weapons. These chemical and biological weapons are perhaps the most terrible weapons in existence. Some kill quick with paralysis and death after brief contact with human flesh, such as chemical nerve agents. Some of these weapons kill slower but just as surely, such as biological toxins. Other toxic agents fall somewhere in between, causing blindness, blisters or other complications.

Biological toxin weapons are agents derived from living organisms such as mushrooms, the skin of amphibian animals, concentrated extracts from castor beans, or shellfish extracts. In addition to being used to produce mass casualties they have often been used to selectively assassinate political threats or opponents.

In Laos in 1976 and in Cambodia (Kampuchea) in 1979, and in Afghanistan in 1979, use of chemical or toxin weapons against the Hmong, Khmer, and Afghans was reported. The reported attacks were often described as an aircraft flying over a village and releasing a cloud that would fall and looked, felt and sounded like rain. The most commonly color was yellow. The substance became known as "Yellow Rain."

The similarities in the descriptions of attacks and subsequent symptoms in Laos, Cambodia and Afghanistan raised suspicions that the same agent was being used. All three locations were linked in some manner to the Soviet Union. In Afghanistan, the Soviets were directly involved in the war, and in Laos and Cambodia, they supported Pathet Lao and Communist Vietnamese forces.[53]

The 1972 Biological and Toxins Weapons Convention (BWC) specifically forbade the stockpiling, acquisition, development or transfer of biological or toxin agents for hostile purposes. The Soviet Union was a party to the BWC at the time of the Yellow Rain allegations.[54]

Thousands were killed by the initially unidentified substances. One former military officer from Cambodia's neighbor, Laos, stated that 1,200 primitive tribesmen in the countryside were killed in these attacks. More died in Cambodia and Afghanistan. Casualties often had horrible skin eruptions and respiratory failure.

The CIA had what it considered very credible evidence concerning Afghanistan:

> A defector, trained in chemical warfare, reports that the Soviets
> used lethal chemicals against Mujahedin in mid-1983 and early 1984

in Ghazni Province, this is the first credible reporting of Soviet use of chemical warfare since February 1983.[55]

The United States determined that toxin weapons were likely being used. US government employees, with the assistance of volunteers and refugees from the affected countries, collected samples for laboratory analysis, acquired medical data on victims, administered questionnaires regarding alleged attacks. The United States continued its investigation through the mid-1980s, collecting and analyzing pertinent information on the alleged attacks. The evidence of toxin weapon use is strong, however to date the US government does not state that the evidence is unequivocal.

In the following chapter we shall consider the struggle in Ireland. According to some, the Soviets had gotten their tentacles wrapped around the Irish Republican Army, whom others call freedom fighters to this day. As with the Palestinian issue, it can be complex to fully understand the situation in Ireland during the Cold War, and the impact of the Cold War on that struggle.

Chapter 5: Cold War Conflict and the IRA

For most of the twentieth century the Irish Republican Army [IRA] and its predecessors fought to liberate the northern six counties of Ireland from British control. There are numerous claims from various authors and witnesses that the IRA had been backed by the Soviet Union in this cause and that factions of the IRA wished to set up a socialist state in all of Ireland. Both sides, including those backed by the British and on the other side those backed by the IRA, accused each other of having instigated the violence that plagued Great Britain and Ireland during the Cold War. It must be noted that Americans provided funds to the Irish through organizations such as Noraid.

Whether the root cause of the troubles in Northern Ireland is land, ideology, or social conditions, the preponderance of the evidence indicates that the Soviets and East Bloc were involved in supporting the IRA. Sinn Fein, an Irish Liberationist political organization that was extremely active in public relations work during the Cold War, states the conflict between Britain and Ireland dates to 1169. Up until that time the Irish were free but after that time the whole of Ireland became a colony of Great Britain. In the early 20th century, through the force of arms, the island was divided into the independent Republic of Ireland in the south consisting of twenty-six counties and six counties that remained under British control, called Northern Ireland. The IRA claimed that there had been clear discrimination against the original Irish holders of this land in the north and sources indicate the Soviets sought to exploit this schism.

According to the CI A' s report on terrorism in 1980, "the Soviets sell [sold] large quantities of arms to Libya—knowing that Libya is a major supporter of terrorist groups.... There has been a clear and consistent pattern of Libyan aid to almost every major international terrorist group, from the Provisional Irish

Republican Army [PIRA] to the Popular Front for the Liberation of Palestine [PFLP]." More specifically the report continued to expound upon IRA activity. "The PIRA has conducted more international terrorist attacks than any other single terrorist group. They routinely attack the British military in Europe."[56] The IRA also repeatedly exploded large bombs in department stores and pubs, killing and maiming many.

There is religious content to this story. The pro-British northern Irish were Protestants and the Irish of southern Ireland and the IRA were Catholics. Politically the IRA was often accused of being leftist or even socialist in its goals and organization. Some say the IRA has gradually moved to the left over the last forty years and was seeking a socialist state in all of Ireland.

In Congressional testimony in 1981, James Billington, Director of the Woodrow Wilson International Center for Scholars, said of the IRA:

> It has not only been subverted and perverted by the left-wing terrorists but it has been taken over by them. The Provisional IRA is now up to no good whatever.[57]

During this period of global Cold War strife, Billington added that in his testimony that:

> ... some IRA guerrillas were trained at Marxist Popular Front for the Liberation of Palestine [PFLP] camps located in Jordan, a fact indicative of IRA links with international terrorism.[58]

In the same 1981 hearing Senator, retired Admiral, and former POW Jeremiah Denton, then the chief champion of terrorism counteraction measures and capabilities for America stated, "Communists always, as a matter of principle, try to exploit any grievance, tension, conflict, violence, they fish in every water. Undoubtedly, there are genuine communists among the Irish, but are there many, or are they merely the loudest and perhaps the most active?"[59]

Stefan Possony, of Stanford University's Hoover Institution, added that there was, within the IRA, in 1981 "...a strong mixture of Marxism-Leninism. The provisional arm of the IRA and elements of the IRA that itself may be serving the world revolution rather than the Irish nation. It is hard to explain their extremism and fanaticism on any other ground." He added that, "The point is that the Soviets play a major role in this business. But they do not exercise a monopoly."[60]

One of the most sensational IRA attacks was the bombing of a fishing boat being used by Lord Louis Mountbatten. He was a cousin of the queen. The bombing took place on August 27, 1979. The Lord, one of his grandsons, and a boat boy were killed by the fifty-pound explosive charge. The IRA claimed full credit for the attack. Reportedly the bomb had been constructed by the Soviet KGB.

Both the Soviets and the US supplied weapons to the IRA Provos. The difference is that Soviet support came from that government. US support for the IRA came in the form of funding from primarily Irish-American immigrants in the US and not the government.[61] There were front organizations operating in the US to support the IRA. In essence, two mortal enemies, the US and the USSR, were supporting the same team in this match.

Evidently the Soviets were winning the struggle for control of the IRA. It did have many stated policies that were clearly socialist. The armed IRA, and the political organization of Sinn Fein, clearly drifted left. Said one observer of the situation:

> The USSR, by means of its training, indoctrination, and other support activities, has managed slowly, relentlessly, to take over—from within—most of the world's major terrorist movements."[62]

While some Americans supported the IRA cause with money and moral support, there was at least one case where the US government sued the IRA support structure in the US. This instance was the case of the *Attorney General of the United States v. The Irish Northern Aid Committee.* The suit took place in 1981 and was settled in the US District Court of the Southern District of New York in April of that year.

The federal court ruled that the weekly newspaper *The Irish People* was connected to the IRA through Noraid and thus the paper was a foreign agent. In the memorandum opinion and order by US District Judge Charles S. Haight, it was ordered that the paper make disclosure of information to the US Attorney General. One witness responded to written questions that the staff of the paper was "doing everything possible to help the Provisional IRA in

Ireland." Another individual testified that "we are fighting a guerrilla war and will continue to do so."[63]

The instance of the IRA in Ireland is a perfect example of one person's terrorist being another' s freedom fighter, as is often the case and certainly was during the Cold War. The IRA was known to maintain contacts with other "liberation" movements around the world including those in Cuba, El Salvador, and Nicaragua. It could be more than a coincidence that a few years after the Soviet Union and global Marxism-Leninism evaporated, to a great extent, serious moves were made towards peace because the IRA had lost its prime backers in the USSR and Eastern Europe [and consequently later lost Libya]. An effective peace was made between Northern Ireland and the Republic of Ireland [the southern counties] with the Belfast Agreement on April, 10, 1998.

Thus far we have examined Soviet state directed terrorism against its own people and other countries. We have also looked at two terrorist groups that had religious ties and motives, as well as motives of regaining "lost" lands. Now we will look at some other groups who were more purely Marxist-Leninist and also had direct and indirect ties to the USSR.

Red Brigades, the Baader-Meinhof Gang/Red Army Faction and Others

During much of the Cold War, in particular during the late stages, US officials gave a light touch when discussing Soviet support for international terrorism. Rather than directly accuse the Soviets of this activity, the statement given was that the Soviets were using surrogates to accomplish their revolutionary dirty work. As we have seen above there is some evidence to the contrary, that is to say that the Soviets did directly support terrorism.

A typical statement by the CIA, taken form an agency "Terrorism Review" dated October 6, 1988, on this topic reads as follows:

> The USSR and Eastern Europe will continue to be unconcerned about end user restrictions on their weapons sales to Middle Eastern terrorist groups and state sponsors. They are not likely to make further counterterrorist concessions.[64]

This consistent position is supported by earlier agency documentation. It is also supported by academic work done since the end of the Cold War. While not the true smoking gun of Soviet involvement in international terror, it does tend to show that "but for" the actions of the Soviets much Cold War terrorism would not have occurred.

In 1981, a CIA report stated that both Germany's Baader-Meinhof group and its follow-on organizations, in addition to the Italian Red Brigades, had been helped with support, such as training, weapons, and asylum, from "Palestinians who had received Soviet training." Even more to the point, and closer to being unequivocal the same report states that, "In sum, the Soviet Union and its allies provide support to groups that have used terrorist tactics in the course of their struggle." The report added that beyond this conclusion, direct Soviet support and orchestration had become "murky."[65]

There was much less equivocation in the 1980 CIA report "Patterns of International Terrorism." The report states that the Soviets support revolutionary violence "is a fundamental element of Leninist ideology." Further the authors of the report state that, "Such violence frequently entails acts of international terrorism."[66]

Outside the issue of support the report states that, "Terrorists have a high rate of success in their operations." This success rate is because during the Cold War the Soviets and their surrogates selected "soft," weak, and most of all unsuspecting targets. "If one person is well protected, terrorists may choose another not as well protected."[67]

The East European connection to terrorism, in particular the Red Brigades, is documented. In addition to being tied to the Soviet-sponsored Italian Communist Party (PCI) for a time, there have been specific references to members of that organization receiving training in Czechoslovakia. Even direct KGB involvement has been brought to the light of day since the end of the Cold War in 1991. As documented in the journal *Modern Italy,* Italian secret service agent Antonino Arconte stated in 2005:

> The Red Brigades were made up of hot-headed students who sincerely believed in revolution through armed struggle, but in their structure were composed of cells...in each of these cells there was a key figure directly in contact with the KGB.[68]

Some examination of what the Italian Red brigades did, in terms of terrorist acts, is in order. Probably the most notorious act they committed was the murder of Aldo Moro. Moro was a former law professor and leader of the Christian Democrat Party. He was a successful politician, if getting elected and reelected is a measure of success. He served as prime minister from 1963-64, 1964-66, 1966-68, 1974-76, and in 1976. In 1978 he was kidnapped and held for two months. He was subsequently murdered by members of the Red Brigades.

In January of 1983, thirty-two members of the Red Brigades were given life sentences for the killing of Moro. This was the stiffest penalty allowed, since Italy had (has) no death penalty. Some of those incarcerated were also guilty of other terrorist crimes.

Another event which got wide coverage on the American media for the Red Brigades was the kidnaping of a US Army General. General James L. Dozier was kidnapped from his home in Verona on December 17, 1981. He was held until January 28, 1982, when he was rescued by the "leatherheads" state anti-terrorist police force.

The Red Brigades claimed credit for a number of other heinous crimes. They claimed to have murdered nine opponents in 1981 and a similar number in 1982. In 1980, the group abducted a high-ranking magistrate. After the terrorists' demands were printed in several newspapers the magistrate was released. At about this time the CIA published a report that read in part: "The Soviets are deeply engaged in support of revolutionary violence, which is a fundamental element of Leninist ideology."[69] The fact that terrorist events were taking place in Italy and elsewhere at the time the research paper was published was probably no coincidence, even if much of the support for terrorism coming from the Soviets was indirect.

Training for all this activity came from Soviet surrogates. In 1985, CIA Director William Casey asserted that forty-four of Italy's most dangerous terrorists were being hosted by Nicaragua and at least six of them were serving as non-commissioned officers in the Sandinista Army.[70] Ties to the global "socialist revolution" predate these relationships by many years.

General Jan Sejna of the Czech army was the highest-ranking communist official to ever defect to the USA. The defection occurred in 1968. Sejna gave up the names of many Italian citizens who were being trained in Czechoslovakia in the 1960s. The training consisted of "exercises in sabotage, use of arms and mortars, guerrilla warfare techniques, and so forth. Let's just say all the trappings of the terrorist…" according to Sejna.[71] Numerous studies indicate these training missions were taking place as early as 1946. Many of the trained terrorists opted to become members of the Red Brigades.

Even the left in the West had no stomach for the Red Brigade tactics. Author Anthony Burgess, though he referred to the murders politely as "naïve dissidents," said of the Red Brigades:

Our Democratic systems may not be working very well indeed, look
at Italy, but they are still preferable to anything the Red Brigades
would install.[72]

The Red Brigades was a resilient organization. There terrorism continued
even as the Cold War began to wind down. In March 1987 they killed an Italian
Air Force general (Licio Giorgieri). The general was working on space
weaponry. While he was driving, two men on a motorcycle pulled up to his car
and shot him dead.

According to further testimony before Congress by Stefan Possony of
Stanford University's Hoover Institution concerning the Baader-Meinhof
gang, its follow-on the Red Army Faction (RAF) and the groups' successor
units have showed surprising longevity during the Cold War. In 1979, an
attempt was made against four-star General Alexander Haig. He was then
NATO Commander and later became Nixon White House Chief of Staff.
Haig went on to be Secretary of State for a short time in the first Reagan
Administration and a candidate for President in 1988. The group Rote Zelle
(Red Cell) which was a follower of the RAF' s path was still operating and they
fired a rocket at Haig' s car. During his tenure as Secretary of State for Reagan
(1981-1982) he pushed for the Administration to "go to the source" of terrorism
in Latin America, namely Cuba.

Also, the El-Fatah-PLO outfits, Spain' s Grapo, and, as we have seen, Italy'
s Red Brigades knew how to survive. In 1990, a shadowy group calling
the "Revolutionary Cells" killed a German industrialist but has not been very
active since. Defections from these groups occurred but they were rare.[73]

Under its leader, Brigitte Mohnhaupt, the German Red Army Faction killed
thirty-four people in the 1970s and 1980s. They staged a series of bank
robberies and kidnappings before dissolving into the Rote Zelle. Mohnhaupt
was given parole from her five life sentences in 2007, after serving twenty-
four years in prison. She is now fifty-seven years old. Many other Faction
members have melted back into German society. On her release Mohnhaupt
had plans to return to being an artist or possibly to work in an automobile
dealership. She had taken over the terrorist organization when its founders,
Ulrike Meinhof and Andreas Baader, committed suicide in 1977.

The Japanese Red Army, a militant Japanese organization, was formed in
1969. The Japanese Red Army undertook several major terrorist operations.

Their goal was to overthrow the Japanese government and to spark world revolution. Their activities included the hijacking of several airliners and bombings. The JRA was also responsible for a massacre at Tel Aviv' s Lod Airport (1972). They also perpetrated the seizure and occupation of embassies in various countries.

The most notorious of the JRA's attacks was the assault on the above-mentioned Israeli Lod Airport on May 30, 1972. The terrorists machine-gunned and bombed the terminal. There were twenty-seven dead and seventy-six wounded.[74] A number of Americans were killed. The group was known for torturing and killing its own members if they felt those individuals were not loyal. The JRA is known to have received Soviet support and weapons that were channeled through Syria and Libya.

General Alexander Haig was on the ultra-leftist target list in 1978, while he was the commander of NATO. As Haig put it there was a real "alphabet soup" of terrorist groups active in Europe at the time. The IRA, Red Brigades in Italy, Baader-Meinhof gang and Red Army Faction (RAF), the Basque ETA all were active. According to Haig there was a "dizzying number of other terrorist groups made up of the bloodthirsty Marxist-Leninist children of the European bourgeoisie" in play as well. On January 25, 1979, despite his heavy security and constant variation of routes and means of transport, his car was attacked with a bomb. It was determined that the communist East German secret police were involved in the plot, as was the PLO; possibly the communist, but not East Bloc Yugoslav government was also involved. KGB training for those involved in the ambush was also strongly suspected according to information provided by an informant. "Nearly all terrorist organizations had some connection to the Palestine Liberation (PLO)," said Haig in his memoir. Testimony of one captured terrorist, Susanne Albrecht, indicated it was the Red Army Faction that had attempted the assassination of General Haig.[75]

Chapter 7: Was There a Plot to Kill Pope John Paul II?

Information profusion and the ability of diverse means of communication amplify the psychological effects of terrorism. In terrorism, it matters much less how many people were killed than how many people are influenced by the death(s). Terrorism during the Cold War was designed to influence both proximate and distant audiences. The assassination of one person can have shattering global impact.

Along these lines, perhaps one of the most vexing issues of the 20th century is, were the communist Bulgarian and Soviet secret services involved in attempting to kill on May 13, 1981, in St. Peter's Square? There is some evidence that this might be the case. Both ideologically and practically there are reasons why the USSR and East Bloc might have wanted John Paul II dead. For the Bulgarians to be acting on the behest of the Soviets would be nothing new in the view of the CIA. In July of 1976 the CIA document entitled "Soviet Strategic Executive Action" stated the background that indicates the assassination may have been planned at the top of the Communist hierarchy. From the document we read:

> The long standing Soviet capability for strategic executive action is not limited to the clandestine paramilitary facilities of the KGB and GRU (Soviet military intelligence), for in the absence of such assets the KGB and GRU can transfer particular assignments to the satellite countries in accordance with a directive relating to

collaboration between the two Soviet services and the satellite intelligence services (secret services of soviet dominated nations).[76]

In March of 2006, the *New York Times* reported that, "top Soviet leaders were behind the failed plot to kill Pope John Paul II in 1981." An Italian commission had come to that conclusion. The report of the commission stated, "This commission holds, beyond and reasonable doubt that the leadership of the Soviet Union took the initiative to eliminate Pope Karol Wojtyia" (John Paul's given name).[77]

In testimony before the US Senate in 1981, Stephen Possony of Stanford said:

> Mehemet Ali Agca who shot, the Pope (sic). He had help and fake documents. Ties of Soviets to assassination attempt—include "the Palestinian organization run by George Habash (PFLP)."[78] ...he did have a Bulgarian pistol. It is improbable that he carried that pistol during two dozen or so border crossings, including bloc border crossings. If he d id not bring the pistol from Turkey or Bulgaria, did he get it into Italy? How?"[79]

Some sources indicate that Agca was involved with both right- and left-wing extremist causes. The Turkish police believe that Agca was moved by a powerful organization. The indicators may point vaguely to the wire-pullers of the Red Brigades; perhaps as a start of new tactics, or a rerun on a bigger scale of the Moro operation. "But such a hypothesis cannot so far be solidified...."[80] Photographic evidence has shown that there was at least one Bulgarian official in the square at the time of the shooting. Further, an Italian terrorist defector identified ties between the PLO, Bulgaria, and the KGB.[81] Agca had mixed with these people in their training camps and bases. Some of the agents in these places also went to the Soviet Union and Syria for training. In 1983, under interrogation from two Turkish judges, Agca admitted to training with Bulgarians and terrorists from around the world in Syria. The training involved weapons, explosives, and political indoctrination.[82]

Moscow almost immediately sought to place blame with the CIA. If it was a communist plot, why would they want to kill the Pope? First, he was Polish and a symbol of freedom to that imprisoned Soviet bloc nation; second, he was the leader of the world's Roman Catholics, and Marxism-Leninism despises religion; and third he was a believer in and a carrier of the message of the freedom of the human spirit.

Some interesting evidence, cited above, on the activity of the KGB during the Cold War has come out of Soviet archives. Thus far we have seen little on this matter from those sources. Perhaps at some future juncture we will know for sure that there was or was not a communist plot to kill John Paul II.

Clearly the Pope was a threat to communism. He was a threat in the sense that he could mobilize mil lions behind the Iron Curtain and particular in Poland. He also had a global audience built in as the head of the Roman Catholic Church. This is reason enough to see why the Bulgarians and Soviets would have *wanted* the Pope dead in 1981. Are this motive and the other evidence available enough to draw the conclusion that they *acted* towards this goal? Many have concluded that this is the case.

Chapter 8: Cold War Terrorism in the Americas

There were violent terrorist groups operating in the United States in the '60s, '70s, and into the 1980s. They were made up mostly of Americans who had at least some university background and often drew support from communist-dominated nations.

For example, on October 20, 1981, twelve terrorists from the Black Liberation Army (BLA) and the Weather Underground Organization (WUO) killed a Brinks guard and wounded two more in an effort to steal $1.6 million. The attack took place in Nyack, New York. Two more police were killed in a shootout five miles down the road. The money was recovered, however, eight of the terrorists escaped.

WUO members also committed bombings at the US Capitol, the Pentagon, and eighteen other targets by March of 1974.[83] Other attacks by the WUO in 1974 included the bombing of the Health Education and Welfare (HEW) building in San Francisco, the bombing of the state attorney general's office, and the bombing of the Anaconda American Brass Company in Oakland, California. A letter of support for another American leftist terrorist group, the Symbionese Liberation Army (SLA) was also issued, and distribution of its propaganda book *Prairie Fire* was also accomplished in this time period.

The WUO was a product of extreme ideological strife between leftist organizations in the US. It broke away from the Students for a Democratic Society (SDS). The SDS had in turn broken away from the Democratic Socialist League for Industrial Democracy in 1963. The Weathermen always insisted that they were not in favor of revolution for the sake of revolution but were leftist idealists searching for a better world. However, they assumed there was no way to reach their goals except for terror.

A slightly different view of the WUO and its origins states that the group was involved with other terrorists and with Cuba almost immediately on its founding. On this subject we might read from the *Congressional Record:*

> The Weather Underground Organization (WUO) in the United States grew out of Cuban influence over a violent faction of the leftists Students for a Democratic Society. WUO began terrorist action in North American cities following guerilla training provided to a group who went to Cuba as a part of the Venceremos Brigade in 1969. A Cuban intelligence officer working through Cuba's delegation to the United Nations became the control operative for WUO's leader, Mark Rudd. The Puerto Rican terrorist pro-independence Armed Forces of National Liberation (FLAN) and Boricua Popular Army (EBP) have also had members trained in Cuba and have drawn political direction and support from the Castro government.[84]

This support from Cuba to North American terrorists came at a time when Cuba was receiving three million dollars each day from the USSR.

The WUO had an extensive propaganda arm. In spite of their trying to intimidate Americans, citizens in the US viewed WUO activity as a rarity or curiosity more than as a real threat. Terrorism during the Cold War, while it happened in the US, was still viewed as something that happened "over there." Events like the Munich Olympics massacre of the Israeli athletes in 1972 only stood out to confirm this impression.

"In one single phrase, the program means this: mobilize the people to fight US imperialism, the common enemy," reads some of the propaganda of the day. "Wage class struggle, fight for socialism. Power to the people," states another WUO leaflet. "Marxism-Leninism is a necessary guide for both understanding the contradictions of class society and developing correct revolutionary strategy," continued the WUO material.[85] In the 1980s, some of the WUO turned and gave information on how the group had operated. Some of the organization was learning in Cuba, for example, how to cause civil disturbances, and then using some of those skills to fan the flames of the 1968 riots at the Democratic National Convention in Chicago.

In 1974, Brian Crozier, Director of the Institute for the Study of Conflict in London, England, stated that "communists from Western and third world countries are being trained in terrorism, sabotage, and guerilla war at a secret school in Moscow." This stops short of proving that WUO personnel were trained in the USSR; however, with the above admissions about Cuba, it is not a far stretch to see that WUO operatives could have been brought to the USSR.

Crozier added that leftist terrorist literature called for attacks on nuclear power stations; stealing of nuclear, biological, and chemical materials; and poisoning the water supplies of large cities. He stated further that "The Weatherman faction has thus far carried out no acts of international consequence, but, the organization is reported to have contacts with two Palestinian groups, Al Fatah and the (Marxists) PFLP, and with the Irish Republican Army."[86]

In the same hearing Senator Strom Thurmond made a brief statement as a member of the committee. He said that, "Authorities seized three cars laden with explosives in a densely populated area of New York City." WMD on American soil was a reality in the 1970s, one that the public largely ignored. After all, the Cold War was in Europe on the borderline between East and West Germany, wasn't it? America was in many respects fortunate during the Cold War. The WUO was dangerous but its actions were somewhat contained, clumsy, and muted. When its issues such as Vietnam and the draft faded away their strength largely, but not completely, drained away.

The United States was far from the only place in the Americas that experienced terrorist violence. Cuba, which went communist in 1959 was, as we have seen in the first volume of this series, was a puppet of the Soviets. This complicity in world revolution was aptly demonstrated in the Cuban Missile Crisis, during which time Cuba' s Fidel Castro allowed the Soviets to turn Cuba into a nuclear base in exchange for aid. By 1981, Castro's Cuba was supporting terrorist violence and/or training in Nicaragua, El Salvador, Guatemala, Costa Rica, Jamaica, Guyana, Grenada, Colombia, Chile, Argentina, and Uruguay.

Dr. Ernesto Che Guevara (1928-1967), was a compatriot of Castro's. Guevara believed that the struggle to bring Marxism to the Americas should take place in the rural areas, 'in the underdeveloped Americas, the countryside must be the basic terrain for the armed struggle."[87] Not all the terrorist communists involved in the Americas agreed with him. After Castro took power he was instrumental in cutting Cuba' s ties with the United States. He redirected commercial ties to the East Bloc instead of the USA. From 1961-65 he served as Cuban minister of industry. After that tour of duty Guevara traveled the world to spread Marxism-Leninism. In 1967, in Bolivia, he was captured, and executed by government troops. Guevara wrote several books on Guerilla Warfare and revolutionary socialism.

Contrary to Guevara's theories about rural revolutionary activity there were a number of events brought about by urban guerillas in the Americas. These included the kidnaping of US Ambassador to Brazil Burke Elbrick in September 1969 by leftist rebels. He was held for approximately three days. The killing of Dan Mitrione of the United States Agency for International Development (USAID) in 1970 was another such event. Additionally in 1970, US Ambassador to Guatemala Gordon Mein was killed in a kidnaping attempt.[88]

We have already touched on the controversy as if it were the Soviet desire for global domination, or the poverty in many parts of the world, that caused many of the leftist terrorist groups to form. Clearly both forces were at play. Terrorism in the wealthy United States tends to show that it was the desire for power that drove the terrorists. Evidence of extreme penury in some places that were fertile ground for the revolutionaries tends to lead to the conclusion that the social conditions provided at least good recruiting ground for the terrorist organizations during the Cold War.

Improvements in education in Latin America increased the number of learned persons in need of employment. It was a cause of rising expectations. The universities and the middle and upper classes are where the terrorists did some of their best recruiting.

Right-wing terrorism was also a problem in the Americas during the Cold War. Both nuns and priests were executed by military death squads that some claim had US training. This is a reverse of the trend for terrorists to be Soviet, Libyan, Syrian, or Cuban trained.

Conclusions: Did We Beat Terrorism or Just Forestall the Inevitable?

One might be able to call the Cold War the first global war on terror. In 1983, there were 2,574 acts of terrorism around the world; in 1984 the number rose to 3,282 attacks, tens of thousands of people were killed. In 1983, the number of Americans killed reached 301. For America this was only a shadow of what was to come on 9/11/2001.

Having earlier said that resources dedicated to the Cold War might have been better used elsewhere, we need to answer the question of whether we should have fought the Cold War at all. Was the cloak of secrecy around so much of US foreign policy necessary? Was it necessary to back the Israelis? Was it this strong alliance with Israel, "American neocolonialism," or the apparent attractiveness of Soviet Marxist-Leninist ideology that "caused" so many volunteer terrorists to join up in fighting Cold War?

We can look at a Christian doctrine on "just war" to see if the West opposing terrorism with force in the Cold War (however ineptly at times) qualifies as legitimate. The doctrine requires these elements:

A just cause,

Legitimate authority,

Right intention,

Likelihood of success, and

The resort to war only as the last resort.

It would seem that the West was on firm ground in all of these areas. Protection of innocents, orders issued by democracies, minimizing collateral damage, superior force available, and the exhaustion of diplomatic means all point to anti-terrorism from the 1950s through the 1990s to have been just.

The question can also be asked if the US saw terrorism during the Cold War in the correct light. The average American, indeed this author, might see the roots of terrorism and the formation of terrorist groups as being poverty, political/civil rights, or land rights. Perhaps because of the dominant political paradigm of what war is we focused too much on the political causes of terrorism during the Cold War. Perhaps this in turn dragged the conflict on longer than it need have been. According to a U S Army War College Strategic Studies Institute monograph:

> Because Americans see insurgency as a form of war and, following Clausewitz, view war as quintessentially political, they focus on the political causes and dimensions of the insurgency. Certainly, insurgency does have an important political component. But that is only part of the picture.[89]

The Cold War was a struggle to the death between the USA and its allies and the USSR and its allies. Stalin predicted this would happen well prior to WWII. It did not turn out as he might have liked however. In 1991 the Soviet Union "died" and the Cold War ended. Of course, today the US, NATO, and UN are left with Cold War remnants turned terrorists to do battle with. Some of them are remnants of guerrilla forces created to fight the Soviets in Afghanistan, some are remnants of forces supported indirectly by the Soviets during the Cold War. It is a complex mosaic of groups and motives that makes up the picture of today's terrorism.

Antiterrorism is not new to the post-9/11 world. After the US Marine barracks in Beirut was attacked by a truck bomb in October 1983, security was enhanced in Washington. The Pentagon had an underpass for vehicular traffic. This was closed to most traffic; barriers went up around D.C. It was nothing like the aftermath of 9/11 but the Reagan Administration had taken notice that such acts could happen on US soil. Anti-terrorism and terrorism counteraction forces created after the Iran hostage crisis were strengthened.

How does all of the information presented here hang together? From looking at early Soviet actions it does not seem to be a case of have's against have not's. The Soviets were not trying to "liberate" people or resources, they were attempting to enslave, terrorize, and conquer.

The Soviets were the original Cold War terrorists, dating to 1917-1918 and their "revolution." A whole new burst of such activity took place dating to the post-WWII period and the conquest of Eastern Europe. The USSR also used terrorism to pose a threat to the Western European nations. Marxist-Leninist doctrines the leadership were espoused by the USSR and spread around the globe. These ideas, backed by force of arms and covert action, were the essence of *global Marxist terrorism*. Surely there would have been terrorism had the USSR never existed, but it would have been a shadow of what the world experienced. Land disputes and lack of basic items of life, such as food and technology, made it easier for the Soviets to do their recruiting and offer, indirect and direct support to terrorists. In the case of post-WWI and post-WWII, direct action by the Soviets is proven.

The targeting of aircraft and how to stop it was often discussed in the West during the Cold War. Aircraft hijackings were seen as only for hostage taking. A problem of countering terrorism was: "commercial aircraft, which not only provide ready-made hostages, but also a place to confine them and means to transport them and their captors anywhere in the world," John E. Karkashran, acting director for combating terrorism, statement September 14, 1977. During the Cold War the terrorist sometimes had the advantage because they chose the time, place, and method of attack. In the post Cold War era this had become yet clearer.

The Cold War was a global civil war of sorts, and terror was often its primary means. Terror was used internally in the communist states and backed externally both directly and indirectly by the communists. It was one camp against the next, often similar to the American Civil War, the world was cleaved into two or three camps. It was a battle for control of a larger society. In the case of the Cold War, it was a global struggle much out pacing the earlier fight in the US.

A few more points will close this work. Many errors could be found that supposedly "led to 9/11" based upon the Cold War handling of terrorism. The intention of this volume is not to point out such things but to give a history of terrorism in its various forms during the Cold War. One item jumps out though. In the 1981 CIA document "Soviet Support for International Revolutionary Violence" the dissemination list is missing at least one significant item. This document is on the level of a "Special National Intelligence Estimate" or SNIE. Nobody in the White House is on the distribution list, not even a junior staffer on the National Security Council Staff. This just serves to demonstrate the lack of importance or priority terrorist activity was given in the government at that time. This is in a way odd, because in 1981 one sees a blossoming of anti-terror reports in government. This is presumably because of the entrance of the Reagan Administration and its at least rhetorically based desire to confront terrorism and its sponsors, chiefly the Soviets.

Perhaps one could say that 9/11 happened because the Cold War was over and the intelligence community had not yet identified fully the new threat. Had the US not fought the Soviets and their minions the results would likely have been even more disastrous than they were. On April 10, 1982, Ronald Reagan signed a then secret National Security Decision Directive (#30) that addressed managing terrorist incidents. Clearly this was forward thinking. The directive brought new organizations into being and stated in part:

> The United States is committed, as a matter of national policy, to oppose terrorism domestically and internationally. Efficient and effective management of terrorist incidents is crucial to this commitment. Successful management of terrorist incidents requires a rapid, effective response, immediate access to institutional expertise, and extensive prior planning. Because of these requirements, the management of terrorist incidents of duration will be handled in the following manner....[90]

The White House document continues on to explain procedures and responsibilities.

In conclusion, the opposition to Soviet support for terrorism was a constant throughout the Cold War. On July 20, 1960, CIA chief Allen Welsh Dulles spoke at a National War College Defense Strategy Seminar. In his secret address he said in part:

> I do not believe that the Soviets now intend to try to achieve their objectives by direct military actions. As long as we maintain our own military strength, they will rattle their atomic missiles from time to tome for blackmailing purposes but probably will not use them.

Hence our attack should be against their economic and subversive thrust into the free and uncommitted world.[91]

Twenty-seven years later Robert M. Gates, then deputy director of the CIA (at this writing he is the Secretary of Defense) spoke to the Dallas Council on World Affairs. He echoed Dulles' comments in stating:

> Throughout the Third World, the Soviet Union and its clients for the past ten years have incited violence and disorder and sponsored subversion.... And, in most instances of state support for terrorism, the government involved is tied in some way to the USSR.[92]

Many topics that have not been discussed here have not because of the sake of brevity. The Iran Hostage Crisis and its leading to new emphasis on special operations, the crisis with Libya over the bombing of the Berlin night club, and many other specifics could have been raised. Some, such as Iran-Contra, were sufficiently raised in volume one of this series. The purpose of this book is to demonstrate that terrorism was a serious problem well before 9/11 and that the Soviets were often the prime instigators of terrorism during the Cold War. Evidence for both of these contentions abounds here and elsewhere.

Statement by a Retired Senior USIA Diplomat

Hi Pat,

Sorry it has taken so long to respond to the chapter in your book—busy times in retirement.

Your mention of the Underwood family is generous and I hope essentially true. If I really said those thoughtful things about the Cold War, it is good to hear there was a time of thoughtfulness.

You may already know much about the operations of USIA, but for future reference, USIA also provided the Voice of America to much of the world in the language of the intended recipients. Radio Marti was beamed at Cuba. From Vienna we printed eight magazines in the languages of Eastern Europe, Yugoslavia and Russia. These were distributed free to the citizens of the countries.

The America House libraries were in the capital cities of the Eastern Bloc countries and were open to all their citizens who wished to read English language books from the US. These libraries also sponsored special events with talks by authors, as well as art exhibits or performances by well-known visiting Americans. We tried to show the true cultural nature of America to people who got only negative information from the government-

controlled information sources of the communist societies. In those days there was some vandalism aimed at the libraries (I still have the burned American flag left in front of Vienna's Amerika Haus Library by a group of protesters against American involvement in Kuwait.)

For my mind, it is a shame we disbanded the USIA at the end of the Cold War. There are still societies that have little appreciation of our culture. Of course the tightly controlled people of the Middle East must be pretty upset that our television shows barely clothed women often in sexual encounters when their women are allowed to expose only their eyes, and a raped woman should be executed because she must have led her rapist to violate her.

Apparently when the leading group begins to lose control, its only recourse is to attack the source of its loss. And if for international political reasons the government cannot declare an open military operation against the source, then what is left is "terrorism" by individuals. Our KKK used the tactic to keep the blacks in place in this country.

Anyway, good luck with the book.
Ron

Bibliography

Government Documents

Casey, William. DCL Remarks at the Fletcher School of Law and Diplomacy: *International Terrorism: Potent Challenge to American Intelligence,* 17 April 1985.

CIA, *The Current Situation in Korea.* 18 March 1948. (secret).

CIA, Directorate of Intelligence, *Communism and Cambodia: Intelligence Report.* May 1972. (secret).

CIA, National Foreign Assessment Center, *The Supporters of International Terrorism,* 29 January 1981. (classification unknown).

CIA, National Foreign Assessment Center, *Patterns of International Terrorism: 1980.* June 1981.

CIA, "Science and Weapons Daily Review" (March 27, 1984): p. 2. (classification unknown).

CIA, *The Soviet Bloc Role in International Terrorism and Revolutionary Violence.* August 1986. (secret).

CIA, *Soviet Strategic Executive Action.* October 1961. CIA,

Terrorism Review. October 6, 1988. (secret).

Dulles, Allen W., *Exploiting the Vulnerabilities of the Communist World.* An address given at the National War College, JuIy 20, 1960. (secret).

Foreign Broadcast Information System, *Trends,* 8 January 1986. (formerly classified confidential).

Robert M. Gates, Address to the Dallas Council on World Affairs, *War by Another Name.* February 3, 1987.

Headquarters, Department of the Army, *FM 100-37-Terrorism Counteraction,* July 1988. (classified, level unknown).

Jenkins, Brian. (CIA), *International Terrorism: Choosing the Right Target.* March 1981.

Metz, Steven, *Rethinking Insurgency.* Strategic Studies Institute: US Army WarCollege2007.

Nixon, Richard. *Public Papers of the Presidents of the United States, 1972.* GPO, Washington, D.C.

US Department of State, *Patterns of Global Terrorism: 1986,* Washington, D.C. January 1988.

United States Senate, 97th Congress. Hearings Before the Subcommittee on Security and Terrorism of the Committee on the Judiciary, *The Historical Antecedents of Soviet Terrorism,* GPO, D.C, 1981.

United States Senate, 86th Congress. Hearing Before the Subcommittee to Investigate the Security Act and Other International Security Laws of the Committee on the Judiciary, *Terrorism in Free Germany: Testimony of Theodor Hans,* GPO, Washington, D.C, 1960.

United States Senate, Report from the Subcommittee on Security and Terrorism, Committee on the Judiciary. *State Sponsored Terrorism, GPO,* Washington, D.C, 1985.

United States Senate, Hearings before the Subcommittee on Security and Terrorism, Committee on the Judiciary. *Terroristic Activity,* GPO, Washington, D.C., 1975.

White House, National Security Decision Directive Number 30, *Managing Terrorist Incidents.* April 10, 1982. p. 1.

Court Documents

Haight, Judge Charles S. Memorandum Opinion and *Order, Attorney General of the US v. Irish Northern Aid Committee* (April 30,1981).

Books

Alexandrov, Victor. *Khrushchev of the Ukraine.* London: Victor Gollancz Ltd, 1957.

Gerringer, Arthur. *Terrorism/Counter-Terrorism Training Manual.* Institute for Strategic Studies on Terrorism, 1985.

Goren, Roberta. *The Soviet Union and Terrorism.* Boston: George, Allen, and Unwin, 1984.

Gross, Feliks. *Violence in Politics: Terror and Political Assassination in Eastern Europe and Russia.* The Hague: Mouton, 1972.

Haig, Alexander. *Inner Circles.* New York, Warner Books, 1992.

Halperin, Ernst, *Terrorism in Latin America,* Sage Publications: Beverly Hills, 1976.

Henze, Paul. *The Plot to Kill the Pope.* New York, Charles Scribner's Sons, 1983.

Livingstone, Neil C. *The War Against Terrorism.* Lexington: D.C. Heath, 1982.

McGuckin, Frank, ed. *Terrorism in the United States.* New York, H.W. Wilson, 1997.

Mickolus, Edward. *Transnational Terrorism: A Chronology of Events, 1968-1979.* Westport: Greenwood Press, 1980.

Rubin, Barry. *Revolution Until Victory: The Politics and History of the PLO.* Cambridge: Harvard University Press, 1994.

Szimski, Bonnie, ed., *Terrorism: Opposing Viewpoints.* St. Paul: Greenhaven Press, 1986.

Trotsky, Leon. *Terrorism and Communism.* An Arbor: University of Michigan, 1961(first published in 1921).

Wardlaw, Grant. *Political Terrorism.* Cambridge: Cambridge University Press, 1982.

Monographs

Ching-Lang, Tsai. *Chinese Communists' Support to Palestinian Guerrilla Organizations.* World Anti Communist League: February 1973.

Metz, Stephen. *Rethinking Insurgency.* Strategic Studies Institute, US Army War College 2007.

Media Sources

Burgess, Anthony. "The Freedom We Have Lost," *Time* 111. May 8, 1978.

CNN World—August 19, 2002.

Fisher, Ian. "Pope's Shooting Laid to Soviets by Italian Panel." A few *York Times,* March 3,2006.

www.state.gov

Journal Articles

Bartali, Roberto. Red Brigades (1969-1974): "An Italian Phenomenon and Product of the Cold War," *Modern Italy* 12, 2007.

Ginat, Rami and Uri Bar-Noi. "Tacit Support for Terrorism, The Rapprochement between the USSR and Palestinian Guerrilla Organizations in the 1967 War." *The Journal of Strategic Studies,* Vol. 30, No. 2 (April 2007).

Endnotes

[1] Arthur Gerringer, *Terrorism/Counter-Terrorism Training Manual*. Institute for Strategic Studies on Terrorism, 1985:1.

[2] United States Senate, 97th Congress. Hearings Before the Subcommittee on Security and Terrorism of the Committee on the Judiciary, *The Historical Antecedents of Soviet Terrorism*, US Government Printing Office, Washington, D.C.,1981:43.

[3] Edward Mickolus, *Transnational Terrorism: A Chronology of Events, 1968-1979*. Westport: Greenwood Press, 1980.

[4] US Department of State, *Patterns of Global Terrorism*: 1986, January 1988, p. 11.

[5] Op. Cit. Senate: *The Historical Antecedents of Soviet Terrorism*: p. 82.

[6] *Ibid*: 12.

[7] CIA, *The Soviet Bloc Role in International Terrorism and Revolutionary Violence* (August 1986): 5. (secret).

[8] CIA—National Foreign Assessment Center, *The Supporters of International Terrorism*, (29 January 1981): 5. (Classification unknown).

[9] Ibid:2,4.

[10] Foreign Broadcast Information System, *Trends*, 8 January 1986 (Confidential).

[11] Headquarters, Department of the Army, *FM 100-37—Terrorism Counteraction, July 1988*, pp. vi, vii (formerly classified, level unknown).

[12] Neil C. Livingstone, *The War Against Terrorism*. Lexington: D.C. Heath, 1982:41.

[13] *Ibid*: 21.

[14] Op. Cit. Senate: *The Historical Antecedents of Soviet Terrorism*: 62.

[15] *Ibid*: 3.

[16] *Ibid*: 18.

[17] Feliks Gross, *Violence in Politics: Terror and Political Assassination* in *Eastern Europe and Russia*. The Hague: Mouton, 1972:11.

[18] Roberta Goren, *The Soviet Union and Terrorism*. Boston: George, Allen, and Unwin (1984): 24.

[19] *Ibid*.

[20] Marc Jensen, *A Show Trial Under Lenin*, The Hague: Martinus Nijhoff Publishers (1982):186.

[21] Leon Trotsky, *Terrorism and Communism*. An Arbor: University of Michigan, 1961 (first published in 1921): 58.

[22] Op. Cit. Goren: 56.

[23] Op. Cit. Trotsky: 58-64.

[24] Victor Alexandrov, *Khrushchev of the Ukraine*. London: Victor Gollancz Ltd (1957): 78.

[25] United States Senate, 86th Congress. "Hearing before the subcommittee to investigate the security act and other international security laws of the Committee on the Judiciary," *Terrorism in Free Germany*: *Testimony of Theodor Hans*, US Government Printing Office, Washington, D.C., 1960:8-9.

[26] *Ibid*: 29.

[21] *Ibid*: 33.

[28] *Ibid*: 1-3.

[29] CIA, The Current Situation in Korea. 18 March (1948): 3. (secret).

[30] *Ibid*: 4, 6.

[31] Barry Rubin, Revolution Until Victory: *The Politics and History of the PLO*. Cambridge: Harvard University Press (1994): ix.

[32] United States Senate, 97th Congress. Hearings Before the Subcommittee on Security and Terrorism of the Committee on the Judiciary, *The Historical Antecedents of Soviet Terrorism*, US Government Printing Office, Washington DC, (1981): 63.

[33] *Ibid*.

[34] *Ibid*.

[35] Bonnie Szimski, ed., *Terrorism: Opposing Viewpoints*. St. Paul: Greenhaven Press (1986): 87.

[36] CNN World—August 19, 2002.

[37] Op. Cit. Szimski: 113-114.

[38] *Ibid.* p. 115

[39] *Ibid*: 121-122.

[40] *Ibid*: 148.

[41] Richard Nixon, Public Papers of the Presidents of the United States, 1972. Washington, D.C.: GPO, (1974): Document287.

[42] *Ibid.* Document 83.

[43] *Ibid.* Document 319.

[44] *Ibid.* Document 319.

[45] Tsai Ching-Lang, Chinese Communists' *Support to Palestinian Guerrilla Organizations*. World Anti Communist League: February 1973. pp. 25-26.

[46] Rami Ginat and Uri Bar-Noi, 'Tacit Support for Terrorism, The Rapprochement between the USSR and Palestinian Guerrilla Organizations in the 1967 War." *The Journal of Strategic Studies* Volume 30, No. 2 (April 2007): 277,282.

[47] Op. Cit, Rubin, ix.

[48] CIA, Directorate of Intelligence, Communism and Cambodia: Intelligence Report. May 1972 (secret): 31.

[49] *Ibid*:47.

[50] *Ibid*:78.

[51] *Ibid*:84.

[52] *Ibid*: 88.

[53] www.state.gov

[54] *Ibid*

[55] CIA, "Science and Weapons Daily Review" (March 27, 1984): p. 2. (classification unknown).

[56] CIA, National Foreign Assessment Center, *Patterns of International Terrorism*: 1980. (June 1981): 9, 13.

[57] Op. Cit. *The Historical Antecedents of Soviet Terrorism*: 26.

[58] *Ibid*: 46.

[59] *Ibid*: 47.

[60] *Ibid*: 48, 45.

[61] Op. Cit. Livingstone: 18.

[62] *Ibid*: 12.

[63] Judge Charles S. Haight, *Memorandum Opinion and Order*, Attorney *General of the US v Irish Northern Aid Committee* (April 30, 1981) 26, 27.

[64] CIA, "Terrorism Review" (October 6, 1988): p. 553. (secret).

[65] Brian Jenkins (CIA), *International Terrorism: Choosing the Right Target* (March 1981): 3.

[66] CIA, National Foreign Assessment Center, *Patterns of International Terrorism*: 1980 (June 1981): 8.

[67] *Ibid*. p. 4

[68] Roberto Bartali, Red Brigades (1969 1974): "An Italian Phenomenon and

Product of the Cold War," Modern Italy 12 (2007): 349-369.

[69] CIA, National Foreign Assessment Center, *Patterns of International Terrorism*: 1980: 8.

[70] William Casey, DCI, Remarks at the Fletcher School of Law and Diplomacy: *International Terrorism: Potent Challenge to American Intelligence*, 17 April 1985:9.

[71] Op. Cit. Bartali: 352.

[72] Anthony Burgess, "The Freedom We Have Lost," *Time* 111 (May 8, 1978): 44-49.

[73] Op. Cit. Senate: *The Historical Antecedents of Soviet Terrorism*. 43.

[74] Grant Wardlaw, *Political Terrorism*. Cambridge: Cambridge University Press (1982):38.

[75] Alexander Haig, *Inner* Circles. New York, Warner Books (1992): 539—543.

[76] CIA, *Soviet Strategic Executive Action*. October 1961:2.

[77] Ian Fisher, "Pope's Shooting Laid to Soviets by Italian Panel." *The New York Times*, March 3, 2006: A6.

[78] Op. Cit. Senate: *The Historical Antecedents of Soviet Terrorism*.: 78

[79] *Ibid*: 79.

[80] *Ibid*.

[82] Paul Henze, *The Plot to Kill the Pope*. New York, Charles Scribner's Sons (1983): 73

[82] *Ibid*: 199.

[83] Frank McGuckin, ed. *Terrorism in the United States*. New York, H.W. Wilson Co. (1997):105.

[84] United States Senate, Report from the Subcommittee on Security and Terrorism, Committee on the Judiciary. *State Sponsored Terrorism*. Washington, DC, GPO (1985):66.

[85] United States Senate, Hearings before the Subcommittee on Security and Terrorism, Committee on the Judiciary. *Terroristic Activity*. Washington, DC, GPO (1975): 541-543.
[86] *Ibid* 210.
[87] Ernst Halperin, *Terrorism in Latin America*, Sage Publications: Beverly Hills (1976): 27.
[88] Ibid. 8-27.
[89] Steven Metz, Rethinking Insurgency. Strategic Studies Institute: US Army War College (2007): 51.
[90] White House, National Security Decision Directive Number 30, *Managing Terrorist Incidents*. April 10, 1982. p. 1.
[91] Allen W. Dulles, *Exploiting the Vulnerabilities of the Communist World*. An address given at the National War College, July 20, 1960. (secret).
[92] Robert M. Gates, Address to the Dallas Council on World Affairs, *War by Another Name*. February 3, 1987.

www.ingramcontent.com/pod-product-compliance
Lightning Source LLC
Chambersburg PA
CBHW052119150726
48002CB00006B/2413